Best Venison Ever

The Indispensable Guide for Big-Game Hunters Who Love Eating Wild Food

John O. Cartier

Published by: Cartier Associates, Inc.
P.O. Box 68, Ludington, MI 49431

Best Venison Ever
The Indispensable Guide for Big-Game Hunters Who Love Eating Wild Food
by John O. Cartier

Brief quotations may be used in critical articles and reviews. For any other reproduction of this book, illustrations and photographs, including electronic, mechanical, photocopying, recording, or other means, written permission must be given by the publisher.

Copyright © 1995 by John O. Cartier
First printing 1995
Printed in the United States of America

Cover photo by Jack W. Cartier
Cover design by John O. Cartier
Layout and design by Kay Richey
Electronically created camera-ready copy by
  KLR Communications, Inc.
  POB 192
  Grawn, MI 49637
Art illustrations by Ed Sutton
  White River Wildlife Art
  3934 N. Riverview Dr.
  Hesperia, MI 49421

Best Venison Ever: The Indispensable Guide for Big-Game Hunters Who Love Eating Wild Food / by John O. Cartier
Venison and Venison recipes - North America

ISBN 0-9647193-0-4

Acknowledgments

Apart from the individuals cited in this book by name, I thank the hundreds or more expert deer hunters, guides, outfitters and chefs who contributed their bits of cooking information that made this book possible.

I want to express my particular thanks to Dave and Kay Richey for their expertise, enthusiasm and perspectives in helping me get this book into print. They are truly experts in the field of publishing outdoor books.

Last but by no means least is Ed Sutton who provided the illustrations. They add a special appeal not found in most wildlife art.

Books by John O. Cartier

1. MODERN WATERFOWLING

2. MODERN DEER HUNTING

3. 20 GREAT TROPHY HUNTS

4. HUNTING NORTH AMERICAN WATERFOWL

5. HOW TO GET YOUR DEER

Information on ordering HOW TO GET YOUR DEER by mail can be obtained by writing: Cartier Associates, Inc., P.O. Box 68, Ludington, MI 49431. Please enclose a stamped, self-addressed envelope. Order blanks and blank pages in back of book are for notes and recipes.

Dedication

To My Wife, Bernice.

Over 20 years ago I dedicated my first book to her because she always read my stuff and offered suggestions, most of which were excellent. In all the years since she has continued to offer ideas that have greatly contributed to the success of each new book.

Contents

Introduction	12
1. Must Know Basics	16
2. Round Steak's Best Bets	25
3. Facts About Roasts	30
4. Dinner In Minutes	37
5. Soups	42
6. Overlooked Super Stews	48
7. Guidelines For Foolproof Barbecuing	55
8. How To Get The Best From Freezers	61
9. Knives — Your Most Important Tools	67
10. Ways To Cook Tough Meat	73
11. Getting The Most From Seasonal Ingredients	81
12. Bits and Pieces Of Helpful Information	88

The Most Important Short Tips
    13-A The Tricks With Gravy   94
    13-B Go With Colorful Cooking   96
    13-C Marinades Make A Big Difference   99
    13-D Where There Is Smoke There's Flavor   103
    13-E The Latest Thoughts On Jerky   107

Introduction

I began my outdoor writing career over 40 years ago. If somebody had told me back then that I'd be writing a big-game cookbook in the 1990's I would have laughed out loud. In those days I didn't know much about cooking, and I wasn't interested in learning many details. My desire was to become the best outdoor writer in the business.

I became good enough to be offered a fulltime job with OUTDOOR LIFE magazine in 1965. As Midwest Field Editor I was assigned writing and editing projects in many sections of North America. Along the way I wrote five books on hunting and many hundreds of magazine articles. All of my writings were published by OUTDOOR LIFE magazine and OUTDOOR LIFE BOOK CLUB. Only one short article had anything to do with game cookery, and most of it was about proper field dressing.

During all those years guides, outfitters and talented hunters wanted to show me a good time when I showed up to write a feature about their area. I ate hundreds of wild game dinners. I marveled at how delicious a few of these meals were, and how poorly others turned out. There were far more bad than excellent, and some meals were downright awful. How would you like to sit down to very overdone caribou steak topped with squirrel-head gravy? The lumps in the gravy

Introduction

weren't potatoes, they were squirrel heads.

Somewhere around 20 years ago it began dawning on me that some of the very best meals were prepared with recipes I'd never heard of. One time on an elk hunt in Montana the fellow I was with brought some venison round steaks to camp. They came from a deer he had shot a week earlier. One night he cut one of those steaks into thin strips and made a stroganoff in almost no time at all. It was excellent.

Over the years I got other great recipes, and they're all in this book. Back in the 70's and 80's I realized that I'd never be able to remember all the tips I got in the field, so I started using a special notebook to record information about food. I still never dreamed of writing a cookbook, I just wanted the recipes for myself.

I took early retirement after I'd put in 20 years with OUTDOOR LIFE, and I developed an obsession for properly preparing game. I had more time to cook, and I had more game to work with. That led to more guests at my house, and the ever increasing realization that friends considered it a real treat to be invited to the Cartier home for game dinners.

One time I broiled some venison steaks for a group. A man who had just celebrated his 75th birthday commented: "I've been hunting deer most of my life. I've cooked tons of venison, but I never had any taste this great. I want your recipe."

After I heard things like that enough times I began thinking that maybe I should do a book that would be a real help to outdoorsmen.

But I made one decision right away. For years I'd been aware that many hunters ruin their meat long before it's cooked. A commercial meat processor would grimace and shake his head in disbelief if he watched how a lot of game is taken care in the field. There is simply no way you can cook a great meal by using inferior quality ingredients. So this book is far less a cookbook than the typical volume loaded with recipes. It's an attempt to offer the really needed advice on wild meat care...plus cooking.

I saw a cookbook one time with a title something like "Six

13

Best Venison Ever

Ingredients Or Less." There were over 250 recipes in that book, and a new edition was published every year for about 10 years. That tells you something. The serious cooks knew how to keep it simple. And "simple" is almost always best when you're cooking wild game. My philosophy is that if something is good, leave it alone. I'd like to think I've been cooking game long enough now to know what works best. I just monitored the best cooks I've met and incorporated some of my own ideas.

Until recently America had this thing that healthy eating is punishment, that it can't taste good and be good for you. Professional lovers of food, who make their living cooking and teaching others how to prepare and appreciate it, have been changing that. They want people to know that game is lean, often lower in cholesterol than other meats, free of steroids and similar drugs, contains less fat, calories and is otherwise just plain good for you.

Ferdinand Metz, President of the Culinary Institute of America in Hyde Park, New York, says: "Cooking technique is of the essence. For example, a perfectly cooked piece of prime meat will still have all the flavors and juices in there. You don't need sauces and other add-ons. Our goal is attractive, tasty food with whole meals totalling no more than 800 to 1,000 calories."

You can do that easily with many various combinations of venison and fresh produce, even if you didn't get your buck last fall. Many non-hunters who appreciate the special taste of venison know that cuts from farm-raised deer are now more available than ever.

I know of one Venison-Of-The-Month Club (Millbrook Venison, Inc. 1-800-774-DEER) that supplies members with various cuts throughout the year. Their venison products are sold nationwide and sent via UPS and 2nd day air. But you pay dearly for this meat. The price for monthly packages for two people is $375, $750 for four per year.

Venison is sold cheaper in ever expanding numbers of specialty butcher shops. In most of these places careful attention is paid to quality control and attractive cuts.

Introduction

There's still another way to eat venison if you didn't get your own. Go to one of the ever increasing numbers of restaurants that feature farm-raised deer meat. Here again, be prepared to pay hefty prices.

Most of us who don't down our own deer have to subscribe to what the old guide said: "The only time venison doesn't taste good is when you ain't got any!"

That's why we can take great pleasure when we are successful in our hunts. There's a sense of celebration that goes with eating our own venison, and knowing that there's a whole lot more in the freezer. It's gourmet subsistence because just having this wild meat provides the presence of special knowledge, skill and persistence. It's a great deal more satisfying than going to the store and buying a prime rib of beef. You're in elite company when you tell the story of how you got your buck.

There's still the job of taking care of the meat in the best ways to get maximum enjoyment from your venison meals. That's what the rest of this book is all about.

Must Know Basics

During my nearly 50 years of big-game hunting I've talked with thousands of deer hunters. Many of those conversations sparked questions about processing and cooking venison. Here are the most frequently asked questions ... and the answers that should do you the most good.

Q. Why aren't my venison chops as tender as lamb chops?

A. Probably because your chops came from a mature deer, while lamb chops come from sheep butchered when they're less than one year old. Harvest young game animals and you'll have tender eating. Table fare fades fast as age increases.

Q. For years I've heard that elk tastes like beef. How come mine doesn't?

A. The flesh of each big game species is much different than commercial meat. Wild game is usually somewhat coarser in texture, dryer when compared to beef or pork, and offers its own unique taste. Game makes great eating on its own merits.

Q. Is boned meat from big game tougher than non-boned meat?

A. Boning tends to decrease tenderness because bones serve as muscle attachments. When a bone is cut out, muscles contract more. This contraction reduces the meat's tenderness. Muscle contraction also explains why the meat from an animal that is killed instantly is more tender than that from a wounded animal that dies slowly. Death under stress always causes muscles to enter into a contracted state. Clean kills produce the most tender meat.

Q. What causes game meat to "sour," sometimes quite rapidly?

A. Heat is the villain. When an animal dies, its organs stop working but its muscle cells don't. They keep producing heat, which in a live animal is carried away by circulating blood. Unless this heat is eliminated by field dressing, the meat will begin to spoil within hours during warm weather. All meat contains bacteria that is kept under control in live animals, but can grow rapidly in dead meat that isn't cooled. The slower the cooling, the faster bacteria grows, especially in meat temperatures above 60 degrees. That's when bacteria multiplies rapidly, creating souring that spreads throughout the meat. Bacteria can't grow in meat that is cooled to about 40 degrees. Field dress your animals as soon as possible, then finish cleaning and chilling the meat within 24 hours. Do this and meat souring will never be a problem.

Q. I've about given up on inviting non-hunting friends for game dinners I cook with prime venison. Too often they don't like it. Is there any way to convince people that this meat is a delicacy?

A. Don't even try. The trick is in knowing who you are cooking for. A friend said recently, "Your charcoaled chops are so good it's a sin!"

"What do you mean, a sin? I responded.

"It's a sin I can't eat 'em more often."

When you know who you're cooking for you won't cook well done pot roast for someone who likes rare chops. Taste preferences vary tremendously.

Q. Why do I often overcook venison even when I exactly

duplicate recipe cooking times?

A. Because it's impossible to tell how long it's going to take to cook your meat. Your stove, charcoal grill, gas grill or whatever may produce more or less heat than mine. You may use more or less charcoal or bottle gas than I do. You may use more or less time to preheat your cooker. There are too many conflicting variables. Experience is the best teacher. Cook the same meats enough times and you'll learn such things as your grill will broil steaks perfectly when you allow five minutes per inch of thickness for each side; or your oven will do a perfect job if you cook a small rolled roast for one hour at 350 degrees. This is the type of knowledge that enables good cooks to turn out superb venison dinners.

Imprint in your mind that published cooking times for grills are vague guidelines at best.

Oven cooking times are a bit more predictable. With an oven preheated to 350 degrees it will take about 20 minutes per pound for rare meat, 25 minutes for medium, and 30 minutes for well done.

Q. Is there any scientific evidence to prove that aging increases the tenderness of venison.

A. A study conducted by the food-technology department at Texas A & M University found that aging retards rigor mortis and extends it over a longer period of time. This process significantly increases the tenderness of venison taken from six study groups involving 30 whitetails. The research also found that aging increases the water-holding capacity of venison and causes the breakdown of muscle fibers. Both factors help increase tenderness. They prove without doubt that aging definitely improves the quality of meat taken from any given animal. Keep in mind, though, that non-aged backstrap meat from a freshly killed yearling doe is going to be a lot more tender than a flank steak from a tough old buck that has been aged properly.

Q. When I dragged my buck out of the swamp it seemed to weigh about 300 pounds. When I got my processed meat back from the butcher it all fit into two little cardboard boxes. How do you explain this?

A. If you put 42 to 45 percent of your deer's field dressed weight on the table you are a good shot and hired a good butcher. If you bone your deer your percentage yield goes down even more. Most hunters don't realize how much "dress-off" there is in all game, their expectations are unrealistically high.

Q. I've heard that game meat should not be washed during the cleaning process. Does this make sense?

A. No. Water in itself doesn't effect meat. Meat processing plants thoroughly wash all carcasses. Game should get the same treatment. Cold water not only cleans meat but helps to cool it.

Q. Should all fat be removed from venison as soon as the carcass is cleaned?

A. No. After skinning leave the heavy layers of fat in place because they help prevent meat from drying. However, fat can turn rancid in storage, and it's usually responsible for the 'gamey' taste some people object to in wild meat. Therefore fat should be trimmed from your meat during butchering, certainly before cooking or freezing.

Q. What does the expert game cook do when faced with frozen leftovers from various venison dinners?

A. Make hash. If the scraps are cooked pieces of prime meat they'll make a hearty and satisfying entree for a light dinner. There's no problem with combining several species of big game. Use one-third cubed meat, one-third cubed potatoes, one-third sliced onions. Season to taste. Or try slicing boned meat into thin strips. Set aside. Saute sliced onions, then mix with frozen green vegetables. Cook until nearly tender. Add meat strips. Saute four minutes. Make combinations of one-third meat, one-third onions, one third peas, broccoli or both. Other good bets: asparagus and corn.

Questions and answers like these emphasize the truism that table qualities of big game can vary enormously. Proper treatment of wild meat takes special knowledge, and there is much more to know than just questions and answers. I could name dozens of examples of how not to take care of game, but a happening last fall serves to highlight the principle.

A friend owns a country grocery store. As a fall sideline, he butchers deer with his meat-cutting equipment. One day I was at his store when two fellows arrived in a pick-up truck. They had two unskinned bucks they wanted processed. It was obvious that both whitetails had been shot several days earlier, and that neither had been properly field dressed. My friend told the men he didn't have time to cut up more deer.

As they drove away Del said, "I'm not going to cut meat that isn't fit to eat. I always refuse to butcher a deer that's into the spoiling stage. The kind of meals those two bucks will produce are going to turn some people into venison haters for life."

All wild game should be finish cleaned the day of kill. All hide and intestines must be removed as soon as possible. This principle is gospel with commercial meat processors.

In slaughterhouses no steer is ever killed, gutted and hung to cool with his hide intact because it's impossible to properly cool carcasses still covered with insulating hides. Automatic conveyors and hydraulic machinery are used to skin cattle and other animals immediately after they are killed. The entire cleaning process is completed so rapidly that steam is rolling off the meat when it's hung in cooling and aging rooms.

While big game is killed by bullets or arrows, commercial animals are killed by methods that don't touch carcasses. None of the meat is smashed or bloodied by gunfire. Bullet-damaged tissue spoils very rapidly even if other cleaning operations are handled properly. Such tissue must be removed in a hurry, and it can't be removed until it's discovered by proper carcass cleaning.

No matter how tender a young deer may be, it will become more tender with aging. Butchers know this, that's why they age prime beef. A temperature range of just above freezing to 38 degrees is perfect. If it gets above 40 degrees I quarter my deer, cut each quarter into chunks and store them in an old refrigerator set for 35 degrees. Venison should age a minimum of five days. I consider one week as ideal. Opening the

Must Know Basics

body cavity fully promotes even aging. I split the pelvic bone and saw through the brisket all the way to the neck. This opens the carcass as wide as it can go.

Everything eventually hinges on cooking meat that is in prime condition. Poorly shot big game has no chance of yielding tender cuts.

Commercial butchers kill their animals instantly. Big-game hunters come close to doing the same by placing their bullets in neck, heart or lung areas. Wait for the close-range shots that make these targets relatively easy to hit. Inaccurate bullet placement can cause high-stress kills which result in strong-tasting and tough meat. Avoid gut shots at all costs.

Once my deer is down I field dress it immediately, being very careful to keep meat free of hair, stomach contents, urine and the likes. I get the carcass home, hung head down in the barn and skinned as soon as possible. I saw off the head, then the front legs just above the knees. Then I finish cleaning the intestinal cavity. Last comes washing the carcass with cold water from a hose. Cold, clean water sloshed from a bucket will serve the same purpose. Always remember that 75 percent of the effort going into preparing truly great game dinners comes before the cooking.

Another overlooked truth is that you DO NOT need complicated recipes to get the most out of game meat. Most dedicated game cooks have tried hundreds of recipes but have settled for a few that produce best results. It's the same principle that works for the expert angler who has hundreds of lures ... but does most of his fishing with a half dozen. The basic elements of cooking game are very simple. You'll always do best if you never underestimate the power of simplicity. All recipes are vague guide-lines at best. Make cooking venison a fun activity. If you don't like rosemary, don't put it in. Use the cooking components you like best.

Don't overlook the fact that bold, sharp flavors harmonize with game. Try sage, garlic, leeks, cranberries, seasoned salts and sharper mustards. Adding herbs and spices will also heighten the flavor of prime meat, in addition to contributing zing to simple cooking methods.

Another roadblock to cooking great game dinners is the myth that all wild meat is tough. Some is and some isn't. The leanest cuts of meat come from those parts of the animal that do the most work. This means legs. The best way to get maximum flavor out of lower-leg cuts is to use them for soup, especially if you make stock first. The long, slow simmering process of making stock not only gets all the flavor out but it tenderizes the meat. Stews make excellent use of tougher cuts, too. So does braising. Much more on this later.

It's imperative to forget the idea that venison isn't table ready unless it's cooked well done. All big game has far less fat than prime foodstore meats. It becomes dry when overcooked, even if it's basted. Except for burgers, stews and pot roasts it's best to cook all big-game meat no more than medium rare. The longer you cook it beyond that stage the tougher it gets and the more it loses flavor.

It's gospel that yearling animals can produce extremely tender and tasty meat. The clean, quick kill of any yearling animal taken in prime habitat produces meat so excellent that it can't be topped in any store. Many hunters never experience eating this marvelous food because they don't pay enough attention to the art of proper meat care.

Now let's dispatch some more myths.

The highlight knowledge of cooking wild game is that those who complain the most know the least about how it should be prepared. Especially those unknowing cooks who believe that all the bad things have to cooked out.

Truly wild meat normally is the purest meat you can eat, and the most untainted by chemicals and preservatives. How you prepare your game from field to table usually determines how successful your meal will be, but not always. Consider the most unfortunate myth of all.

MYTH: Meat from big-game animals is always gamey. It tastes strong and it's tough.

FACT: Some wild meat will be lousy no matter how well it's cared for. Unlike domestic meat animals that can be raised and fed to produce maximum flavor and tenderness, game can be inferior for many reasons we can't control.

Old age is a top offender. Any meat from game that is past it's prime age is going to tough and stringy. Diet is another factor that can turn potentially great dinners into very poor fare.

Then there's the rut. Bulls and bucks that are crazy with the breeding urge never make tender eating. I've been hunting for over 50 years, so I no longer try for trophy animals. Now I want to harvest the best table fare I can get.

I don't think one hunter in 100 truly appreciates the fact that cleaned game meat stored at temperatures higher than 40 degrees is getting 'stronger' tasting by the hour. Outside the kitchen, heat and meat do not mix.

MYTH: You can't tell the quality of meat by looking at its fat.

FACT: The color of fat offers a great quality clue. The lighter colored the fat the better the quality of the meat. Yellowish or brownish fat signals poor quality. White fat signals the best quality. In any event, trimming fat from cleaned meat doesn't get the attention it should. While domestic meats have saturated fats, wild animals have unsaturated fats. This unsaturated fat is strong flavored. Most of it should be cut away before it affects the taste of the meat.

It's an easy job because big-game species have their fatty deposits located just under the skin rather than being marbled throughout the meat. It takes only a few minutes to cut major layers of fat off steaks, chops and roasts before eating or freezing.

MYTH: It's okay to grind venison into deerburger before shipping.

FACT: Freshly butchered steaks, roasts and chops will keep fine for several days if properly cooled, but ground meat spoils very rapidly. First, it warms from going through the grinder. Even if the resulting pile of burger is refrigerated the meat in the center of the pile won't get cooled. At best, freeze all burger from big game as soon as possible after grinding. At worse, spread the meat out on foil in your refrigerator so it

Best Venison Ever

all cools evenly, then freeze within days.

MYTH: You can put frozen meat on the grill or in the oven with no adverse cooking effects. You'll get the same results as with thawed meat, with the exception that it will take longer to cook.

FACT: Venison tastes better when thawed before cooking, for several reasons. Thawed meat absorbs seasonings more efficiently, thereby improving flavor and texture. Thawed meat retains juiciness and cooks evenly. It also permits use of a meat thermometer for accurate cooking. If you must cook frozen meat choose burgers other thin pieces that will thaw and cook through in a hurry.

THE BIGGEST MYTH OF ALL: The hunt is over when big game hits the ground dead.

FACT: The hunt is over when you've just finished eating another superb meal of properly prepared and cooked wild meat.

Round Steak's Best Bets

A well shot and properly butchered deer will yield more pounds of round steak than most other cuts. You can do great things with round if you appreciate the nature of this meat.

All cuts with "round" or "loin" in the name (sirloin, tenderloin, eye of round, bottom round and top round) are the leanest cuts. Combine this knowledge with the fact that venison doesn't have any inner-marbling fat as beef does. A cut of beef will baste itself internally while it's cooking. Venison can't do this, so it's very easily overcooked.

Each round steak comes from the deer's hind leg, but the upper portion of the leg is much more tender than the lower part. The farther down the leg, the less tender the meat. Leave the lower leg for stew and stroganoff; and the shank parts for burger, soup, sausage, jerky or braising.

Cooking magazines these days feature venison as the gourmet food of the 90s. Cooked properly, round steak can be even more gourmet than many other cuts, but the margin for error is narrow.

The biggest sins are overcooking and the use of too many complicated sauces and marinades. Round steak cooked beyond the medium-rare stage is tough. Too many condiments destroy the delicate flavor of venison.

Best Venison Ever

   I cut my round steaks 1-1/2 inches thick. Thinner steaks are too easy to overcook. Many game recipes call for 1/2-inch thick steaks. It's extremely difficult to cook such a thin piece of meat any way except well done. Thin cuts normally will be browned from the outside to the center. They will be tough, dry, and lack in flavor. It's hard to ruin a 1-1/2-inch steak this way. The ideal is to achieve a rich brown on the outside and a juicy, pink middle that oozes the unique venison flavor.

   The internal temperature of rare is 140 degrees. Medium done is 150 degrees, and well-done is 165 degrees. There isn't much difference between these numbers, and that's why it's so easy to overcook. Always remember that you can cook underdone steaks more, but you can never cook overdone meat less.

   Top round is the most tender part of each round steak. In beef this cut is often labeled "London Broil" and is sold at prices as high as sirloin and prime rib. This surprising fact implies that top round can be every bit as tender as venison chops. Most hunters will find this truth a bit hard to accept, especially those who still believe the preposterous notion that all venison has to be fully cooked before it's ready to eat.

   Beware of the recipe that tells you exactly how long to cook steak. But you can't fail if you make a small incision into your steak and check the stage of doneness when you think it's about rare. You lose minimal juice with this cut, and it's guaranteed to tell you exactly how much your meat has cooked.

   Like all wild game, venison is tight-grained. This means that the meat is bound to be tougher than choice domestic meat that is bred and fed for tenderness. I tenderize my round steak in two ways.

   The Jaccard Corporation, 3421 Benzig Rd., Orchard Park, NY 14127, manufactures a simple mini meat tenderizer that's really great for tenderizing steak. It's a mechanical gadget that consists of 16 sharp spring-loaded blades that pierce tiny, closely-spaced holes through the meat. You can pierce hundreds of muscle-cutting holes in your steak in minutes.

   Marinades can do a further job of tenderizing. Italian Wishbone salad dressing is the simplest and one of the best I've found. The only

Round Steak's Best Bets

other precooking preparation I do is the removal of the silverskin and other tissue from the outside edge of the steak. This is imperative for overall tenderness.

My easiest recipe is the one I use most. Put 1/4-cup Italian dressing into a heavy-duty plastic freezer bag big enough to easily hold an average round steak. Add steak. Seal bag, agitate dressing around meat, place in refrigerator for at least two hours; overnight is ideal. Take meat out of bag in time for it to reach room temperature (promotes even cooking) and pat semi-dry with paper toweling. Grill over high charcoal or gas heat for 4 to 6 minutes on each side. Slice across the grain in thin strips and serve hot on heated plates.

That's all there is to it. No mess, no dirty pans, no grease. Do not salt meat prior to cooking. Salting tends to absorb the juices you want to preserve. Add seasonings when steak is half cooked.

I'll talk about kabobs in detail in a later chapter, but I want to mention here that they are made to order for round steak. The following serves four.

    1 pound marinated round steak cut into 1-1/2-inch cubes
    2 small zucchini cut into 1/2-inch chunks
    4 medium onions, quartered
    1 green pepper cut into 1-inch pieces
    1 cup large mushroom caps sliced in half

On eight skewers alternately thread all ingredients. Broil on covered grill about four inches from heat source for roughly six to ten minutes, turning twice. For spicier kabobs, substitute red pepper for green, and 1/2 cup inexpensive red wine for the marinade. The acid in wine does a fine job of tenderizing, especially for someone who doesn't like Italian dressing. Always use red wine for any type of dark meat.

Try the following if you like rice and insist on well-cooked meat.

    1 whole round steak...marinated
    2 tablespoons vegetable oil
    2 large onions

Best Venison Ever

    1 can mushroom soup
    1/2 cup red wine
    4 servings cooked wild rice

Cut steak into thin strips across grain. In large skillet brown meat in oil. While meat is browning slice onions into 1/4-inch rings and add to skillet. Saute until onions are tender. Blend soup and wine. Pour over steak. Reduce heat, cover and simmer for 1/2 hour. Serve over bed of fluffy rice. Mashed potatoes or noodles can be substituted. Serves four.

Venison stew has been a staple in deer-hunting camps throughout history, but it has a reputation for utilizing just about any cuts of less-tender meat. Stews make fine use of round steak.

    2 pounds venison cut into 1-1/2-inch cubes
    1 large onion peeled and sliced
    3 carrots pared and chunked
    2 celery stalks, sliced
    3 medium potatoes, pared and quartered
    1/3 cup all purpose flour
    2 garlic cloves, chopped
    2 cups Burgundy
    3 tablespoons vegetable oil
    1 tablespoon fine herbs

Dredge round steak cubes in flour and brown in large skillet. Mix Burgundy with two cups water and pour over meat. Add onion, garlic and herbs. Simmer one hour. Add carrots, celery and potatoes. Simmer for two hours, less if vegetables become tender. Serve over dumplings, biscuits or top-quality bread cut into thick slices. Serves four to six.

Top quality, flavorful and robust bread is back in style after many decades of wimpy substitutes. Good sturdy bread is great for preparing theater steak, the elegant all-in-one-dish meal utilizing round. Serves four.

    1 round steak cut into four servings
    3 tablespoons Crisco
    2 large onions cut in 1/4-inch rings

Round Steak's Best Bets

1/2 pound mushrooms, sliced
4 thick slices robust white bread

Melt Crisco in large skillet. When hot, add onions and cook about two minutes. Add mushrooms and cook one more minute stirring constantly. Set aside. Fry meat quickly on medium heat to desired doneness.

Remove steak from skillet and keep warm with vegetables. Quickly fry bread, turning over once, so all pan juices are sopped up. Place a slice of bread on each plate, divide and arrange onions and mushrooms on bread. Place steak sections on top and firmly press down with spatula. The object is to get warm juices oozing down into the vegetable. Serve immediately, while still warm.

Facts About Roasts

A prime deer contains many delicious cuts, but roasts offer so many distinct advantages they're favorites with most experienced cooks. Roasts are the flannel sheets and down comforters of the venison scene because they're big and offer several successive meals of prime meat. They are intensely flavored and meld perfectly with fresh vegetables, gravies, and cold glasses of whatever matches your tastes. Leftovers are excellent. Reheating often improves flavors.

A slice of perfectly cooked roast can vary from rare to well done and still be as simple and savory as meat can get because it can be cooked to match anybody's taste preference. It's good to know though that some cuts lend themselves to given methods of cooking.

Venison chuck, for example, comes from the deer's shoulder and is made up of several muscles having varying degrees of toughness. Front shoulder meat averages 20 percent of the animal's carcass. It's ideal for pot roast because moist cooking methods ensure that all tougher cuts become as tender as possible. You can also help cut down on toughness by marinating the roast before cooking. Put the meat in a glass bowl, pour a half cup of your favorite marinade over it, rub it in while turning and then refrigerate for at least four hours. Here are the recipes that work best for me.

SIMPLE POT ROAST

    1 chuck roast, 2 - 3 pounds
    2 tablespoons vegetable oil
    1 pint frozen or canned tomatoes
    1 medium onion, sliced

Wipe remaining marinade off roast then sear all sides in hot skillet to seal in flavors. Layer onion in bottom of Crockpot or other slow cooker. Place meat on onions and cover with tomatoes. Roast on high for one hour, then reduce heat to low. Cook 6 to 8 hours. Season to taste. Serves six. (Variation: substitute one envelope dry onion soup mix combined with one can cream of mushroom soup for tomatoes.)

PRISTINE POT ROAST

    1 chuck roast, 3 - 4 pounds
    2 tablespoons vegetable oil
    2 medium onions, peeled and quartered
    3 cups carrots, chunked
    1 cup celery, chunked
    1 bay leaf

Wipe marinade off roast then sear. Preheat oven to 300 degrees. Roast meat for three hours, turning occasionally. During last 40 minutes add vegetables and season roast to taste. Make gravy. Remove bay leaf. Serves six or seven.

Rules of thumb: It takes about 45 minutes per pound to cook pot roast in oven preheated to 300 degrees. They become as savory as they can get when they're slowly simmered in their own natural juices and flavored with about 2 cups of red wine, beef stock or bouillon.

The most remarkable roasts are the tender cuts that are cooked rare to medium rare. Rib-eye roasts are the greatest, but any cuts containing meat close to the ribs make excellent eating. Next best are rump roasts. The rump roast that comes off the top of the hind leg — the cut that's created in preparing the leg for cutting round steaks — is one of my favorites. Any roast coming from the rump area can be excellent if not overcooked. Several recipes work equally well.

RUMP ROAST #1

> 1 rump roast, 2 - 3 pounds
> 2 tablespoons vegetable oil
> 2 cloves garlic
> 1/2 package dry onion soup mix
> seasonings of choice

Preheat oven to 350 degrees. Rub roast with oil. Cut garlic cloves into 8 slivers. Cut 1/2-inch deep slits into meat in eight scattered places. Stuff each slit with a sliver of garlic. Put roast on rack in shallow pan. Sprinkle dry onion soup mix on top of meat. Roast 20 minutes per pound for rare. Season during last 15 minutes of cooking. Serves six.

RUMP ROAST #2

> 1 small rump roast, 1 1/2 - 2 pounds
> 2 tablespoons vegetable oil
> 1 medium onion, chopped
> 1 cup dry red wine
> 1/2 cup venison stock or broth
> 1/2 teaspoon thyme
> 1 bay leaf
> 2 tablespoons butter

Preheat oven to 450 degrees. Lightly sprinkle seasoning salt on all sides of roast and rub with 1 tablespoon oil. Put meat in shallow pan...do not use rack but rub rest of oil on pan to prevent sticking. Cover with onions. Roast 30 minutes. While meat is cooking mix wine, stock, thyme and bay leaf. Cook over high heat for about five minutes. Swirl in the butter. Discard bay leaf. Pour sauce over roast during last 10 minutes of cooking. Serves four.

Simpler variation: Rub roast with oil, sprinkle with 1/4-teaspoon thyme and dash of garlic powder. Forget the sauce.

RIB-EYE ROAST

1 rib-eye roast, any desired size from 1 to 5 pounds
1 to 5 cloves garlic, crushed
1/4 to 1 teaspoon thyme
1 teaspoon to 1/3 cup red current jelly
1/4 to 1 cup venison stock
1/4 to 1 teaspoon dry mustard

Preheat oven to 350 degrees. Rub garlic over surface of roast. Put meat on rack in shallow pan. Roast 20 minutes per pound for rare. While cooking, combine thyme, jelly, stock and mustard in small saucepan. Cook about 5 minutes, stirring occasionally until bubbly. Pour over roast during last few minutes of cooking.

HERB ROAST

1 3-pound rump, loin or rib roast
1 tablespoon vegetable oil
1/4 cup flour
2 teaspoons marjoram
1/2 teaspoon thyme
2 teaspoons rosemary
1 clove garlic, crushed
1 cup apple juice
1 cup water

Preheat oven to 325 degrees. Cut 1/2-inch deep slits in several places on meat. Rub roast with oil. Combine next five ingredients, pat mixture on meat and stuff into slits. Pour apple juice and water into shallow roasting pan. Set roast in liquid...no rack. In slow oven, preheated to 325 degrees, cook roast 25 minutes per pound. Keep basting about every 15 minutes. Five to six servings.

CAMP ROAST

1 eight to 10 pound roast
1 apple, sliced
1 package dry onion soup mix

Worcestershire sauce
1/2 cup water

Make a paste of onion soup mix and water. Layer apple slices on top of meat and cover with paste. Sprinkle with Worcestershire sauce. Put meat on rack in shallow roasting pan. Set oven for 250 degrees. Go hunting and let roast cook for 6 to 7 hours. If desired, add barbecue sauce or otherwise season to taste. Serves about 12. This roast has a touch of tradition that will rekindle memories of past great hunts.

Any roast goes great with baked potatoes, butternut or buttercup squash, and tossed salad. Use French bread for sopping up juices. Another excellent vegetable combination is steamed string beans mixed with sauted morel mushrooms.

DELIGHTS OF ROLLED ROASTS

The advantages of rolled roasts may be the best kept secret of big-game cookery. These roasts can be cooked to the same degree of tenderness as prime rib of beef, they are easy to construct, easy to cook, carve and serve. They make great leftovers. Most of these roasts are made from the tenderest part of the hind quarter, the upper part of the thigh.

Begin your butchering session by removing the rump-roast section from the top of the hind quarter. Now you have a whole hind leg ready for the traditional cutting of large diameter round steaks. Instead of cutting a 1-1/2 inch steak, make your cut five to eight inches wide. Do this by cutting across all muscle groups (top round, eye of round and bottom round) down to the thigh bone. Make the complete cut by circling around the bone with your knife, then make the perpendicular cut by sliding the tip of your knife and blade along the center line of the bone to the top of the leg.

You now have a thick chunk of meat ready to butterfly into several thinner sections all connected with roughly inch-thick hinges. Do this by continuing your perpendicular cut down to a hinge of meat one-inch thick. Stop the cut and open the meat so it lies flat. Swivel your knife blade 90 degrees and make a horizontal cut out to within one inch of the end of the slab. Repeat this cut with the remaining thick half. The result is a slab of meat about one-inch thick and approximately 12 to 15-inches long. Smaller roasts require one less horizontal cut.

Now roll the meat tightly while tucking in any edges that are sticking out. Using a five-foot length of cord, tie a tight loop around the edge of the roll farthest away from you on your work station. Next, make a loop wide enough to slip over the roast. Make a single twist in the cord and secure the loop snugly around the roast about one inch from the tied cord at the far end. Continue making these snug loops about one inch apart with the last one about an inch from the closest end of your roast. Run the remaining cord under the roast and out the far end. Snug and tie both ends of the cord together on top of the roast at top of first loop you tied. Snip loose ends of cord and discard.

These directions ARE NOT carved in stone. Any boned piece of meat that is thick enough to butterfly into a one-inch slab at least six or seven inches long can be rolled and tied into a roast. Last fall my son and I cut and tied several very small roasts by using a different — but popular method — of boning the meat from hind legs. The key to success with this system is knowing how to remove the top round and bottom round sections from the rest of the leg meat.

First cut through the thin layer of silverskin that covers the leg. Make your cut from the knee all the way up the leg. Work your fingers into the natural seam that separates the top round from the rest of the leg. Pull vigorously. You'll find that you can almost pull the top round free from the rest of the meat. Little knife work is needed until you get to the back of the leg. Here you'll have to cut along the bone to completely remove the entire top round. This section makes excellent rolled roasts.

You can also make rolled roasts from what's left of the thigh...bottom round and sirloin tip. These two muscle groups can be partially separated by pulling apart at the natural seam, then cutting the meat away from the bone. These meat sections are great for making small rolled roasts. If you want the biggest roast you have to go with the method I described earlier, cutting across all muscle groups.

I preheat my oven to 350 degrees, rub cooking oil and sprinkle dry onion soup mix over the meat, insert a few slivers of garlic into slits cut into the roast, then cook for one hour. This gives medium-rare meat in an average roast. For any size roast figure 20 minutes per pound for rare to about 35 minutes for well done.

Dinner In Minutes

It so happens that big-game meat lends itself to fast and easy dinners because it cooks in a hurry. It also so happens that speed is foremost among the demands of American cooks today.

According to Good Housekeeping Institute's Food Trends Study, 86 percent of active cooks want main dishes that can be prepared in 30 minutes or less. Three of the simplest and quickest cooking methods - broiling, sauteing and stir-frying - easily meet this restriction provided some of the work is finished in advance. One-Pot wonders also fill the bill. So will a ragout or a sandwich of substance, which is something you can sink your teeth into and taste in layers. Such a production really is not a sandwich, it's a meal all in itself and can serve for a hurry-up supper loaded with nutrients.

My favorite 30-minute meal is broiled venison chops. Put the frozen meat packages in your refrigerator so they'll thaw by the time you're ready to cook. At that time ignite your gas grill and set temperature knob to high. During the 10 minutes it takes your grill to reach high heat, scrub baking potatoes and put in microwave. Put the chops on grill. While they're broiling, make a tossed salad. You should have a meal fit for a king in no more than 30 minutes. This is no misprint. According to very old cookbooks venison had long been considered the meat of kings. So not only did you get dinner in a hurry, you got one of the best possible meals available to big-game hunters.

Sauteing is to French cooking what stir-frying is to Chinese, a time-honored quick-cooking technique. The primary difference between sauteing and stir-frying is in the fat used, sauteing requires very little. It's also easy, efficient, and it preserves the crisp textures of vegetables while producing intense flavors.

A large, heavy-bottomed skillet with high, sloping sides and a long handle that stays cool works best. Heavy pans create an even heat that browns food evenly. Pans with the newer non-stick coating are okay, but they tend to pool the oil in one location.

With either cooking method organization is all important because the ingredients cook so quickly. It's essential that preparations be finished before you begin to cook. Pat food dry before adding to hot fat to prevent excess sputtering and steaming. Cut meat and other foods into thin, uniform strips.

High heat is essential to sear food. Unless you begin with a very hot pan you cannot stir-fry or saute successfully. Stir-frying over low heat makes mush. Heat the pan over high heat until a drop of water sizzles and evaporates immediately. Then add just enough oil to coat the bottom of the pan lightly. Test its heat by dropping in a small bit of the food you are cooking. It should sizzle and sear immediately.

Cook food in small batches. If you crowd the food it will steam rather than develop crisp edges. Allow pan to return to full heat between batches, add a bit of oil if necessary. Like frying fish, you have to stand over the skillet, constantly jockeying the contents, moving the heat up and down, removing and adding food and paying strict attention to detail. If you don't want to learn how to do all this work, spare yourself the exercise and use an easier cooking method. But if you really must have dinner in minutes, sometimes even in seconds, this is one of the best ways to go. Most modern cookbooks offer dozens of recipes for stir-frying or sauteing. Anything that works for beef or pork will work fine for venison.

Dinner In Minutes

A carefully stocked pantry is one key to cooking delicious dinners in a hurry. A fine selection of canned goods should include beef and chicken broth for quick soups and stew ingredients. Creamed corn and seasoned potatoes are good bets. Use canned quick appetizers too, such as pitted olives, sardines, pickles and fruit cocktails.

Of most importance is a well-stocked freezer. Tops on the list are frozen chops, steaks, roasts and hamburgers. Next come vegetables that freeze well. The best include winter squash, broccoli, spinach, chard, tomatoes, corn and peas. Frozen bread and rolls are always handy. Use combinations of almost any of these frozen items to make complete meals.

Thawing first in the microwave saves time too, easily chopping 20 to 30 minutes off the clock. You can call home from work and have someone thaw your chosen dinner items, then they're ready for cooking when you arrive.

Frozen One-Pot Wonders can be great time savers in several ways. Stews, ragouts and casseroles can be prepared for weekend main dinner; then leftovers are frozen for future lunches. Try this venison roast:

> 2 pounds baking potatoes, peeled and sliced thinly
> 2 large onions, sliced thinly
> 1/2 pound sliced red peppers
> 1 cup dry white wine
> 1/4 cup olive oil
> 4 garlic cloves
> 1 4-pound roast, bone in

Rub bottom of casserole with 1/2-clove garlic, then put in potatoes in layers. Chop remaining garlic cloves and spread one-third over potatoes. Layer on sliced onions and another one-third garlic. Layer peppers and remaining garlic on top. Pour wine over everything, then oil. Place sturdy oven rack directly above other items. Season roast, then place on rack so that meat juices will drip on layered foods.

Roast uncovered at 400 degrees for one-half hour. Reduce heat to 350 degrees and continue roasting 1 1/2 hours for rare. Turn venison every 15 minutes, basting from liquid underneath. To serve, carve roast in thin slices and arrange on warm serving platter, then surround with mixed vegetables gratin. Makes six servings. This is the most time-saving roast I've ever cooked from scratch. Leftovers can be used for sandwiches of substance, or other great lunches.

Here's a venison ragout that's quick and easy. It's often referred to in old cookbooks as "The Stew of Kings."

> 2 pounds venison stew meat, trimmed and cut into 1 1/2-inch cubes
> 2 tablespoons butter
> 2 tablespoons oil
> 1 large onion sliced thinly
> 2 cloves garlic, minced
> 1 1/4 cups red wine
> 1 1/4 cups beef broth
> 1 cup dried cranberries
> 1/2 pound small mushrooms trimmed and quartered (use wild in season)
> 1 teaspoon sugar

Heat two teaspoons each of butter and oil in skillet. When very hot stir-fry meat in two batches on all sides. Add same measure of butter and oil for second batch. Cook about one minute for each batch. Place seared meat in 1 1/2-quart casserole.

Heat more butter and oil to medium high, two teaspoons each. Saute onions and garlic four minutes. Add wine, broth, cranberries and sugar. Bring to boil. Pour over venison. Toss to mix well.

Bake one hour at 350 degrees. Add mushrooms. Mix well. Bake 30 minutes more. Season to taste. Serve hot, spooned over a wide variety of bases such as mashed potatoes, noodles, rice, a combination of chunked and cooked carrots, celery and potatoes, or Texas toast. The basic ragout freezes extremely well, mostly because it doesn't contain potatoes which always turn mushy after freezing. Each original combination serves six. I often double or triple the basic ragout ingredients, cook and freeze them in various size batches. The reheated ragouts make great meals with freshly-cooked vegetables, or sandwiches of substance without. Such meals can be prepared in minutes with microwave ovens.

Slow cooking would seem to be out of place in our fast-food world, but it's actually one of the quickest ways to get several dinners in minutes. These meals originate as stews or casseroles put together during leisure times and slow cooked for six to 10 hours. Crockpots and other slow cookers do the job. They are great for all of us who want to eat well and cook good food without a lot of fuss. See chapter 10 for details.

The last and one of the best ways to get quick meals is to cook a big venison roast on a slow off-season weekend. Sunday's roast becomes sandwiches to go with hearty soup on Monday, and hash with tossed salad on Tuesday.

Leftovers from most any big meal often make quick stir-fries. You can use leftover meat, vegetables, bread and even some appetizers. This is why stir-frying may be the most popular quick-cooking method in the world.

Soups

Picture this: You've finished a morning's hunt with two companions. You open the door of the cabin and turn the stove burner to high under a big pot of homemade soup. By the time it's simmering your buddies have a large fire crackling in the fireplace. The delicious aroma of hearty soup mixes with the pleasant smell of burning firewood. You know that you're just moments away from a really great chill-eliminating treat. A morning like that is about as good as life gets.

Soup that you make yourself can easily be a meal when served with thick slices of robust bread. They're filling enough to satisfy any outdoorsman, whether or not he has been hunting.

The making for the following recipes were gathered from the best outdoorsmen cooks I've met across North America. They all agree that soup is the greatest remedy for utilizing most any type of big-game scraps, leftovers, or even choice cuts. And you don't have to be cold to appreciate these classics in your kitchen. Richly satisfying, soup can be as enjoyable to make as it is to eat year around.

Soups can be easily put together with a minimum amount of work. And, unlike many other recipes, you can make excellent soups without following instructions to the letter. Some good soups materialize out of experimenting. It's very possible that each batch will taste a bit different and still be superb. As in all cooking though, there is no way the end result can be excellent unless the ingredients are the best quality. Great soups are easy to make from scratch only if you work with great materials. Knowledge of some basics will help.

Soups typically run about 90 percent water. That's not nearly as thin as it may sound when we realize that a hamburger is 50 percent water. The high water content does not limit a soup's nutritiousness. The water and fat of the broth capture the vitamins and minerals released by vegetables during cooking. In fact, you'll get more nourishment from potatoes, carrots and other vegetables cooked in a soup than from those boiled and eaten plain. This further points out soup can make a full meal when eaten with whole-grain bread. A tossed salad of fresh lettuce and other garden produce is another top side dish.

Americans consume more than 10 billion bowls of soup each year, and 99 percent of households buy soup. That emphasizes their popularity, even when they aren't very good. Home made game soups can be so superior to the canned varieties that there's no comparison. We truly have gourmet eating when we correctly put together our own quality ingredients.

Soup has also been shown to be an effective food for weight control. Because it's hot it demands the eater's attention, and it requires the use of a spoon. Both factors help slow the eating process. In a report published in the "Journal of the American Dietetic Association" these qualities play an important role in successful weight loss and maintenance.

The best soups begin with bones cooked slowly in water over low heat. Simmer long enough to draw out the flavor, usually a minimum of four hours. I leave some meat on the bones for additional flavor. If you have your big game butchered by a professional meat cutter be sure to tell him to save the shank and other bones he would normally strip clear for hamburger meat. Tell him to leave a bit of meat on those bones. Deer hunters who bone their own meat and discard the bones are wasting some of the best possible soup ingredients.

After cooking the bones and skimming off top scum during the process, pour the broth through a fine sieve. This makes sure that bone slivers and chips, plus whatever other unwanted materials, don't get into

43

the finished product. I then chill the broth until the fat congeals. It's easy to remove in solid form.

Vegetables should be added to the broth in sequence. Each type has a different cooking time. Onions take the longest to cook, so they go into the reheated stock first. Then comes celery, carrots and turnips, broccoli and cauliflower, and so forth. Potatoes always go in last because they cook in a hurry.

Leftovers from previous meals make fine ingredients, but be sure to add them just before the cooking is finished. Remember that leftovers have already been cooked once. All you want to do now is heat them to the temperature of the rest of the just cooked ingredients. Overcooked leftovers can be bad news for an otherwise delicious soup.

When you're building soups it's very important to add only the vegetables that you and your family like. If a person dislikes cauliflower, for example, he won't like your soup if it contains this item no matter how perfect you may think it is. As with all foods, appetites vary greatly between individuals. Your favorite soup may rank way down the list with me, and vice versa.

Lastly, for the preliminaries, frozen soups are not nearly as good as those made fresh. Any food item that is cooked correctly, cooled and frozen, and later reheated is bound to lose a lot of quality. Textures of cooked foods break down during the freezing process. This is especially true with vegetables. Cooked potatoes freeze so poorly they always turn mushy when reheated. It's always best to make just enough soup to last a few days. Save your freezer space for foods that lose little or no quality while freezing.

Let's start cooking with the most basic game soup recipe. You can use this one with just about any big-game meat. Slight variations can turn this venison soup into elk, moose, caribou or whatever soup.

VENISON SOUP

    1 large, or 2 or 3 small soup bones with 1 to 2 pounds of meat. (Meat may be attached to bones or may be scraps.)
    1 large onion, diced

2 celery ribs, chopped
3 carrots, chopped
4 medium potatoes, diced
1 pint canned tomatoes
2 beef bouillon cubes
1/8 teaspoon crushed thyme
2 bay leaves

Put bones and meat into a large pot and add enough water (three to four quarts) to cover. Bring to a boil. Add one slice of onion and bay leaves. Cover and simmer about four hours. Six hours won't hurt. Some cooks insist on 10 hours, but it just isn't necessary from my experience. Let broth cool.

Remove hardened fat, then strain broth and discard onion and bay leaves. Remove meat from bones and return meat to pot. Discard bones. Bring broth to a boil. Add onions and carrots. Cook at simmer for 15 minutes. Add celery, simmer for 10 more minutes. Add potatoes and continue simmering for 15 minutes. Add beef bouillon cubes, canned or frozen tomatoes, and thyme. Simmer 10 minutes while adding whatever seasonings you may want to use. Serves six to eight.

I go very light on seasonings while cooking. It's mostly a personal choice as to how much salt, pepper, oregano or whatever to use. Soups can be seasoned at the last simmering before eating, and each cook can be his own judge.

Vegetable contents can be changed to suit personal tastes, and also seasonal availability. The first crops to mature in my big garden are peas. They go great in any meat soups. So does broccoli and snap beans. Properly stored, potatoes from my garden last almost all year. If I don't have them I substitute noodles, cooked according to the directions on the package. There are all kinds of substitution possibilities.

Here are a few cooking tips to rely on until they become second nature. While everything is on the stove your soup will "cook down" to ever lower volume because the liquid steams and evaporates. When your soup is finished you should have about one quart of liquid per cup of meat. As evaporation takes place you'll have to add a little water to make up the difference.

Any soup garnished with parsley adds a bit of taste and a lot of eye appeal. Let your imagination run wild as far as meat ingredients go. There is no hard and fast rule. If it's good quality meat it will make good quality soup. Use beef bouillon cubes for all big-game soups.

If you do a lot of hunting you're bound to get some big game showing considerable bullet-damaged meat. Such meat is not suitable for attractive cooking cuts but it's ideal soup meat. It has to be washed, then cooked thoroughly so you can separate bone chips and whatever from the broth. Simply cook and pour through a sieve. Cut the usable meat into bite-size chunks and check thoroughly for additional waste before returning chunks to broth.

There are two schools of thought on soups — the broth lovers and the vegetables lovers. My wife likes soup so thick I often tell her: "That's not soup, it's stew." Take your choice. It's easy to thicken soup by "cooking down" to any thickness consistency you want. If the broth lover's soup gets too thick he can thin it by adding any desired amount of water or stock.

As a rule of thumb, one quart of soup serves four.

Any recipe that calls for water will be improved if stock is substituted, or just about any combination of stock and water.

RICH GAME STOCK

    3 pounds bones cut into 3-inch pieces
    1 pound scrap meat attached to bones, or separate pieces
    2 medium onions peeled and quartered
    1 stalk celery cut into 2-inch lengths
    2 medium carrots pared and cut into 2-inch lengths

Place bones and meat into large pot and cover with water. Bring to boil, reduce heat and simmer two hours. Skim impurities from surface occasionally. Add more water to cover, simmer two more hours. Add vegetables, simmer one more hour. Strain stock through fine sieve into large bowl. Discard all solids. Refrigerate over night. Skim congealed fat from surface, leaving just enough to add a bit of flavor. Make soup immediately or freeze stock in plastic containers of suitable size for your family's soup needs.

The finer the mesh of your sieve, the smoother your stock. If you don't have a fine sieve, use an ordinary one lined with a layer of wet, wrung-out cheesecloth.

There are no hard and fast rules for any stock. The more bones the richer the stock. The key principle is that the very best soups begin with bones cooked slowly in water over low heat long enough to draw out the best flavors.

If you butcher your own deer and bone the meat, consider the advantages of making six months supply of stock at one time. As you bone the meat, put the bones into a very large kettle. Add water to cover. Put in three large onions, peeled and quartered, plus three chunked celery stalks. Simmer 4 to 6 hours, adding water when necessary. Cool overnight. Remove and discard hardened fat and vegetables. Strain. Freeze in plastic containers large enough to hold the stock you normally use for your average size batch of soup.

Overlooked Super Stews

There are so many magical advantages to stew that it's time to change the image of this one-dish meal. It's made to order for the end of hunting seasons when weather is turning into winter, and there's plenty of game on hand. What could taste better and be more satisfying than a hot, hearty and rich stew on a cold and blustery evening.

One-dish dinners are also a welcome change from time-consuming cooking chores. Another great advantage is that you can cook one stew and use the leftovers for a second quick meal. For these double-header recipes, serve half and refrigerate or freeze the rest. For example, use what's left of a venison stew to make a quick venison pot pie. All you have to do is stir up a simple sauce, add the leftovers, add some mushrooms and peas, then cook until bubbly. Pour the works into a casserole, top with biscuits and bake 10 minutes. There are many such variations for any stew.

Most flesh parts of big game can be used for stew if the meat can be cut into stew-size pieces.

A further plus is that game meat is perfect for stews. The leanest and toughest cuts are simmered slowly to tenderize as much as possible. Slow cooking stew also keeps vegetables from getting mushy. Your favorite game meats and vegetables simmered in succulent sauces and spiced to perfection is a cooking job made to order for stew.

Still another success secret is to use a heavy pot, the heavier the better. The old-fashioned cast-iron pot with a cast-iron lid, such as a Dutch oven, is one of the best. The thick iron distributes the heat evenly, thereby producing uniform cooking and eliminating hot spots that cause scorching. Heavy-duty electric frying pans are good bets, too.

Vegetables that hold their form when cooked are best for stews. Carrots, potatoes, onions, celery, green beans, peas, brussels sprouts, whole-kernel corn, turnips and parsnips are standard ingredients. The most appealing stews don't contain vegetables that turn soft when cooked. Cabbage, chard, spinach and others are more suited for soup. Although most stews contain potatoes, they can overcook and turn mushy while cooking unattended for many hours.

A good variation is to omit potatoes and serve your stew over rice. Potatoes aren't a good ingredient for doubleheader recipes because leftover spuds don't freeze well. They also cook much faster than other vegetables. To get the best tasting and firmest potatoes in stew, cook them separately and mix in when the other ingredients are nearly done.

Gone are the old days when stew was snubbed as a simple way to use up last week's leftovers. Today, when prepared by imaginative cooks using the best recipes, the possibilities for big-game stew are tremendous.

VENISON STEW # 1

1 1/2 pounds venison, cut into 1 1/2 - inch chunks.
2 tablespoons flour
1 teaspoon salt, (I use seasoned)
1/4 teaspoon pepper
1/4 teaspoon thyme
1 large onion, chopped
1 package gravy mix (brown)
2 cups water
4 medium potatoes, quartered
3 carrots, peeled and cut into 1-inch pieces
1 turnip, peeled and diced
6 tablespoons margarine

Dredge chunks of meat in flour mixed with salt, pepper and thyme. Set aside. Saute onion in three tablespoons margarine until soft. Add remaining margarine and brown meat. Combine gravy mix with water. Bring resulting liquid to boil, then reduce heat. Combine everything except potatoes, simmer 20 minutes. Add potatoes and simmer 30 minutes, or until vegetables are tender. Makes 4 servings. Variation: Omit potatoes and serve over noodles, or rice, especially if you double quantities of ingredients for doubleheader dinners.

VENISON STEW # 2

1 1/2 pounds venison, cut into 1-1/2 inch chunks
6 medium potatoes, cut into chunks
6 brussels sprouts, cut in halves
3 celery stalks, cut into 1-inch pieces
1 envelope, dry onion-soup mix
1 pint canned tomatoes (containing at least 1 cup liquid)
1 1/2 cups sliced mushrooms

Preheat oven to 350 degrees. Place venison, potatoes, carrots, celery and brussels sprouts into casserole dish. Sprinkle with onion soup mix and favorite seasonings. Add tomatoes and mushrooms. Cover tightly with aluminum foil and lid. Bake 1 1/2 hours. Makes 4 to 6 servings.

VENISON STEW # 3

1 1/2 pounds venison, cut into 1 1/2-inch chunks
1 1/2 cups water
1 teaspoon salt (seasoned)
1/8 teaspoon pepper
1/2 cup dry red wine
4 medium carrots, cut into thirds
4 medium potatoes, cubed
1 cup fresh or frozen cranberries
1 medium onion, chopped

1 stalk celery, cut into pieces
1 clove garlic, minced
2 tablespoons Worcestershire sauce
2 whole cloves
1 bay leaf
1/2 cup water
1/4 cup rye flour

In Dutch oven combine stew meat with water, salt and pepper. Bring to boil. Reduce heat; cover and simmer 1 1/2 hours. Stir in wine, carrots, potatoes, cranberries, onions, celery, garlic, Worcestershire sauce, cloves and bay leaf. Cover and simmer for 45 minutes or until vegetables are tender. Combine the 1/2 cup water and rye flour, stir into stew. Cook and stir until thickened and bubbly. Remove bay leaf. Serve with wild rice.

VENISON STEW # 4

1 1/2 pounds venison, cut into 1 1/2-inch chunks
2 1/2 tablespoons cooking oil
1 large onion, chopped
1 complete celery stalk with leaves, cut into 1-inch chunks
1 small green pepper, chopped
1 clove garlic, sliced thinly
1 cup venison stock (may substitute can of beef broth)
1 cup canned tomatoes
1 teaspoon soy sauce
1 teaspoon seasoned salt
1 1/2 tablespoons paprika
2 tablespoons fry mix flour
6 medium potatoes, cut into chunks
6 carrots, cut into chunks

Shake meat cubes in paper bag with flour, paprika, seasoned salt and garlic slices. Brown meat cubes in oil. (Note: cubes for any stew should never be crowded while browning. It's better to brown them in relays than to have them touching. They won't brown properly if crowded.) Set aside.

Add onions, green pepper and celery. Saute about eight minutes, return cubes. Add remaining ingredients and bring to quick boil. Turn heat to low. Simmer for 1 1/2 hours. Stir occasionally. Serves four.

A guide I met once claimed his cider stew was the best stew going. It makes an excellent meal, and offers an interesting switch on occasion. Mix 2 cups apple cider or apple juice, 1/2 cup water and 1 tablespoon white vinegar. Bring to a boil. Cool, then stir into stew about one hour before other ingredients finish cooking.

VENISON STEW # 5

1 1/2 pounds venison, cut into 1 1/2-inch chunks
1 large onion, chopped
1 cup celery, diced
1/2 cup uncooked rice
1 can cream of chicken soup
1 can cream of mushroom soup
1 can mushroom stems and pieces
3 teaspoons soy sauce
Salt and pepper to taste
1 cup peas
1 cup water

Brown venison, onion and celery in margarine. Mix together and add rice, canned soups, mushrooms, soy sauce, and seasonings. Place in casserole. Add 1 cup peas and 1 cup water. Bake at 350 degrees until rice and meat are tender, about 1 1/2 hours.

BIG VENISON STEWS

Cooks in hunting camps often make huge stews to feed a dozen or more hunters. I often make big batches too, then store several frozen meals. Remember though, that cooked potatoes turn mushy when frozen. Omit the potatoes in any stew or soup that's going into the freezer. Here's a good all-around recipe.

>5 lbs. venison cut into 1 1/2-inch chunks
>1 quart stock
>1 quart canned tomatoes
>3 ounces flour
>3 cloves garlic
>1/2 lbs. celery cut into 3/4-inch pieces
>1 lb. onions cut into 3/4-inch pieces
>3 tablespoons oil
>1 teaspoon thyme
>2 bay leaves
>1 teaspoon salt (seasoned)
>2 teaspoons Worcestershire sauce
>1 lb. carrots peeled and cut into 3/4-inch pieces
>1 lb. potatoes peeled and cut into chunks

Brown meat chunks in cooking oil. Remove, leaving oil in pot. Add onions, celery, and garlic to pot and cook until tender. Place flour in pot, stirring well. Gradually add boiling water or stock and stir until thick and smooth. Add tomatoes, spices and browned venison. Stir until well mixed. Reduce heat and simmer uncovered 1 1/4 hours, stirring occasionally. Add carrots and cook 30 minutes more, covered. Add potatoes, cook 20 minutes more. Remove bay leaves. Serves 15.

QUICK AND EASY VENISON STEWS

>1 1/2 pounds venison, cut into 1 1/2-inch chunks, then browned
>1 pound can each of diced carrots, drained small whole onion, drained; whole tomatoes, peas, drained; cut green beans, drained; small whole potatoes, drained
>1/2 can beef consomme
>1/4 cup quick-cooking tapioca
>1 tablespoon brown sugar
>1 bay leaf

1/2 cup dry white wine
1/2 teaspoon seasoned salt
Pepper to taste

Combine everything, mix well, cover and cook on low for eight to 10 hours. Makes six to eight servings.

Another quick deal involving almost no preparation involves frozen vegetables. Buy a package of frozen stew vegetables, put in pot with browned venison chunks, turn to low heat and leave for work. When you return home your main dish will be ready.

You can substitute any big-game meat for all the recipes mentioned. All one-dish meals may be enhanced a great deal with a tossed salad and French bread.

Guidelines For Foolproof Barbecuing

Most of us will testify to being barbecue experts. Still, our irresistible urges to grill often result in inferior meals. The reason is that outdoor grilling appears to involve little more than lighting a fire and cooking meat over it.

It ain't so. The best grilling results involve specific procedures. The barbecue isn't just for burgers and hot dogs anymore, it's a great tool for year-around cooking of a variety of foods. Close attention to details will help you avoid disappointing yourself and your guests when cooking venison, Following are the absolutes that should always be followed.

Most grilling debates are usually between charcoal and gas. Understanding the features and benefits of different grill designs can help you make the right choice if you're going to cook with just one grill. It's helpful to know that blind taste tests have proven that there is no significant taste difference in foods cooked on charcoal or gas grills.

The big advantage with charcoal is the wider range of less expensive grills. They are also lighter weight and easy to move. Disadvantages are building a fire each time you cook, then waiting about 30 minutes for the fire to reach cooking temperature.

Gas grills are easy to ignite, preheat to cooking temperature in

10 minutes, are inexpensive to operate, offer easy cleanup and are more convenient. So convenient that I use my charcoal grill about once a month. One or both of my gas grills are usually used several times a week during good weather, and at least once a week during winter.

Both types of grills efficiently handle direct or indirect cooking. With the direct method, food is placed directly above the heat source and must be turned one or more times to expose the surface of both sides of the meat to direct heat. This is the fastest cooking process.

With the indirect method foods are cooked by reflected heat, like in a convection oven. Grills with covers are necessary as foods are cooked for longer times at lower temperatures. Covers insure juicier meats without turning because heat circulates around all surfaces of the food. This method is best by far for large cuts including all types of roasts.

Lack of maintaining correct cooking temperature is the major error with either method. Correct procedure begins with starting the fire.

CHARCOAL: Remove the grill lid and open all dampers. Arrange about 50 briquets in pyramid-shaped mound on center of fire grate for an average size (22 1/2-inch) kettle grill. Ignite with charcoal starter. Let the briquets burn 20 to 35 minutes before putting any meat on the grill. Coals are usually ready when covered with a light grey ash, an indication of an even cooking temperature. An excellent test involves spreading out the coals evenly, then holding your hand, palm side down, at grate height above the fire. Count the seconds you can hold your hand in this position before extreme heat forces you to jerk it away. Two seconds indicates that the fire is very hot, three seconds medium hot, four seconds medium. Five seconds indicates a low fire, too low for fast cooking.

Leave the coals spread evenly for the direct method of cooking. For indirect cooking move half the coals to the left side of the fire grate, half to the right side. Close the dampers half way.

With charcoal, the original 50 briquets will produce even heat for about 50 minutes. Then add eight briquets to each side, repeat every

Guidelines For Foolproof Barbecuing

45 minutes. It's easy to do this if you position the cooking grate with handles over coals so additional briquets can be added through openings beneath the handles. Charcoal requires oxygen to burn, so make sure nothing clogs the vents (dampers) at any setting. This is easily done if accumulated ashes are removed before starting each new fire.

GAS: Maintaining correct cooking temperatures with gas grills requires no more than turning the temperature knobs. For indirect cooking both knobs are set on high for preheating, then one burner is turned off. The biggest mistake is not knowing when the grill's cooking temperature had reached the point called for in any given recipe. The best technique is using a standard stove oven thermometer for either type grill when using the indirect cooking method. Place the thermometer over the unlit burner when using a gas grill, over the center section of a charcoal grill, or on the warming rack if your grill has one. Adjust heat settings to maintain correct temperatures.

Experience with your grill will tell you how long to cook various cuts at what temperatures during various times of the year. (Cooking times will be shorter at an outside temperature of 80 degrees than at zero). Here are general guidelines. A medium heat setting suitable for most thick cuts and roasts is 325 degrees to 375 degrees F. A high heat is best for steaks, chops, hamburgers and kabobs. Always preheat grills before starting to cook. When possible let meat come to room temperature before cooking, this promotes even cooking.

Grill hamburgers about 12 minutes at medium to medium-high heat. Turn over once. One to 1 1/2-inch steaks or chops will be rare in six to eight minutes; cook another two minutes for medium-rare; 10-12 minutes medium. Turn twice. Grill flat meats between 3 and 5 inches from heat source.

Roasts should cook at high heat for about 15 minutes to sear, then at around 350 degrees. The rule to follow is total cooking time of 20 minutes per pound before testing for doneness. Always remember that big-game meat is leaner than beef or lamb. It becomes tough and dry if cooked too much. It's far better on the rare side than overcooked. Good insurance is a meat thermometer.

Speed is important when grilling. If the broiler is not hot enough, too many juices will escape before the food is cooked. Always heat the grill to high before adding food. Then adjust heat according to your thermometer.

While broiling, use a small, clean pastry brush to brush the surface of the food frequently with a small amount of oil. This prevents lean meat from drying out.

The trickiest part of grilling is knowing when the food is done. To test steaks and chops by touch, press the meat lightly with the first two fingers. Very rare meat is soft and pulpy. Rare gives easily when touched. It is seared, but no juices appear on the surface. Medium meat feels firmer and has juices appearing on the surface. Well-done meat is firm, does not yield to pressure and is covered with juices.

You'll know for sure how much your meat is cooked if you make a small incision with a fillet knife when a touch test indicates that the meat is cooked to the rare stage. Visual inspection is positive, and almost no juices will be lost through a tiny cut. Always remember that undercooked can be grilled more, but overcooked can never be cooked less.

All meat is not created equal, even from the same animal. Cut steaks and chops at least one-inch thick, thinner cuts dry out too quickly. A 1 1/2-inch steak is gourmet. Use tongs instead of large forks to turn meat as piercing causes juices to flow out. Salt draws moisture out of meat while cooking, so use it for seasoning only when cooking is half finished. Never attempt to tenderize meat in salt water, it will only toughen it.

The external fat of venison and all big game is tallowy and strong-tasting. Most of it should be trimmed during butchering, or at least before cooking. Trimming fat also keeps flare-up flames to a minimum. A disadvantage is that broiled, trimmed and lean game meat dries out rapidly after cooking. Another answer to this problem is serving game as soon as possible after cooking. While it's true that the flavor and carving ease of prime beef and domestic fowl is enhanced by standing 20 minutes after cooking, the opposite is true with venison and

Guidelines For Foolproof Barbecuing

all big game. This is a very important rule to remember.

Any outdoor cook who takes pride in his results will want to own the proper utensils to make the job easier. Tongs, spatula and wire brush (brass bristles are best) should all be long handled for easy use near hot fires. Metal and/or wooden skewers are a must for preparing kabobs. Use wooden skewers for kabobs that have short cooking time. Soak them in water for 30 minutes before adding food, then they won't burn when placed on a hot grate.

A handy item is a grill-safe skillet. It can be used for frying, baking, warming sauces, simmering stews or making gravies. Just as handy is a shelf cutting board on front or side of your grill. It keeps seasonings and grilling utensils within easy reach.

Keeping your grill clean is essential for efficient operation, but like all the other tips I've offered in this chapter, it's nowhere near as complicated as most grilling instructions claim. Before cooking spray the cold grill grate with a nonstick vegetable oil. After cooking but while grate is still warm, sprinkle dry baking soda on a damp sponge and lightly scour grate, then scrub with your grill brush. Occasionally, after fats and juices accumulate on the lava rocks of a gas grill, turn them over when the grill is cool. Replace the grate, turn the burners to high, ignite and close the cover. The lava rocks and grate will self-clean in 15 minutes. Cooking grates on charcoal grills need only a scrub with your grill brush after each fire.

GENERAL TIPS: High heat to sear, low heat to penetrate. Always start cooking on high heat (your thermometer should register about 500 degrees) then adjust vents or burners to achieve temperature your recipe calls for.

Choose a grill site that has easy access to your kitchen, that's sheltered from prevailing winds, yet is a safe distance from objects that might catch fire.

Lava rocks should be spread in a single, even layer.

Any 3 to 5-pound big-game roast will cook in less than 2 hours on a covered grill, and that's for medium to well done. It's best to set a timer for 1 1/2 hours because it's easy to forget how fast meat cooks on either charcoal or gas grills.

Trimmed excess fat from meat can be used to lightly grease cooking grates.

It's a simple matter to put a side dish on the grill near the main course. Foil wrapped or skewered vegetables add special flavors to any grilled venison meal. Other side dishes, including casseroles, may be prepared in advance in the kitchen, then reheated on the grill. Butter bread or rolls, seal in foil and heat. But don't go overboard, foods on a crowded cooking grate require more time than just a few foods.

Charcoal grills almost never wear out. Gas gills have more and weaker parts, making them subject to faster deterioration. If you've looked everywhere and still can't find a part for your gas grill, try Grill Parts Distributors, 6150 49th St., St. Petersburg, FL 33709. They have parts for almost every grill ever manufactured. Phone 1-800-447-4557, 8-5 weekdays.

How To Get The Best From Freezers

HOW wild food is frozen is as essential to its fresh and delightful flavor as HOW it is cleaned and cooked.

Though the freezer is the BACKBONE of home storage systems, it isn't a simple system. There are rules to follow to achieve maximum success.

Always freeze realistically. Select your best quality big game. Only the best is good enough for the finest dinners. Freezing can never improve the quality of food. Resist the temptation to freeze inferior-quality meat just because it's there and you have a lot of it at the moment. While it's true that the operating cost of freezers are less at three-quarters full than three-quarters empty, there may be bonanza harvest days ahead. It's poor planning to have to eat successive meals of top-quality meat because your freezer is full. There are several ways to lick the problem.

As a general rule, don't freeze more than you can use in one year. Harvest cycles come and go in one year's time, and the sooner frozen food is used the more likely its best quality will be retained. However, this principle is certainly not carved in stone. Commercial meat producers sell consumers more meat only after the buyer has consumed most previous purchases. This is why freezer storage times published by commercial meat interests seldom exceed 10 months.

The key is in proper wrapping. Many outdoorsmen spend hours properly cleaning their game, then hurriedly place it in any handy plastic bag and put it in the freezer. The best quality meat can't be kept well this way. If it's correctly frozen it can retain quality far longer than commercially recommended storage times.

The major problem in quality freezing is the presence of air in the wrappings. Direct contact between frozen flesh and air creates freezer burn. Eliminate the air and you'll eliminate the dehydration that causes freezer burn. The best way to do this is to freeze big-game cuts in water so that the meat and water combination completely fills sealed plastic freezer bags. If the contents of the bag are 100 percent meat and water there's no way that air can get to the contents.

The disadvantage of this method is that meat frozen in a protective bath of water takes up a lot of freezer space.

The next best bet (the one used by most hunters) is to protect the meat with tight, multiple wrappings of top quality materials designed specifically for freezer use. You can almost completely eliminate air from pieces of boned meat. These soft and pliable chunks of meat can be molded to almost any size or shape. I use Freezer Loc plastic for the initial wrappings. Cling Strips are embedded in this material to make it cling tightly and seal tightly. It's thicker than ordinary foil, and is more tear and puncture resistant.

Begin by placing the meat to be frozen on the center of a large piece of plastic wrap. Bring the end of the wrap nearest you over the meat. Then fold both sides over the center, squeezing the plastic against the meat as you work. Roll the bundle of meat, squeezing air out of the package as you go, to within six inches of the end of the plastic. Fold the end of the wrap over on itself, and press it firmly against the meat. You now have your meat packaged as air free as it can possibly get without freezing in water.

I always double wrap or double bag all my packages for two reasons. First is the insurance against accidental punctures, plus the fact that two airtight wrappings have double the protection against freezer burn. Then there's the necessity of labeling each package with precise identification of contents. It's difficult to write on plastic wrap, but easy to work with waterproof marker pens on freezer paper, freezer tape, or freezer bags incorporating write-on areas.

Lay your package of plastic-wrapped meat about two-thirds of the distance to the center of a large piece of heavy-duty (shiny side up) freezer paper. Bring both ends of the paper together above your meat. Make a fold about one inch wide that folds both edges of the paper together. Continue making this fold until the last one ends up tight against the meat. Tape fold tightly. Now fold one end of loose freezer paper in upon itself from each side until you have a triangle shape of folded paper. Fold this bundle once and pull it tightly against the original fold that holds the meat. Secure firmly with tape. Repeat with the other end of loose paper.

This process of wrapping is well known as the drugstore fold.

I use it for most of my cut big-game meat harboring bones. It can accommodate odd-shaped cuts and those roasts or other chunks of meat having exposed edges of sharp bones. Pad the sharp edges with little clumps of foil, then press a large sheet of foil around the entire piece of meat to eliminate air pockets. Use the drugstore fold with freezer paper to double seal the entire package.

Flat, envelope-type freezer bags (such as Ziploc) are excellent for freezing small cutup sections of game. Greatest storage life is achieved by freezing this meat in water. But you can save freezer space by eliminating the water and immersing the meat filled bag into a container of cold water before sealing. Simply immerse the bag up to the zip-like closure. Water pressure forces all air out of the bag before sealing.

It's common practice to freeze game pieces in water filled waxed dairy cartons, but I quit that practice long ago. These cartons have to be thoroughly washed, you need a scissors or knife to trim cartons at ice level, a band of freezer tape must be applied to the carton for identification marking, and any open container leads to rapid evaporation of protective ice covers. Go with plastic wrap, heavy-duty freezer paper and plastic bags and you go with the best.

There are several rules to follow if you're going to freeze a large amount of meat at one time. At least 24 hours before the meat is to go into your freezer, turn the temperature-control dial to maximum coldness. Scatter the newly-wrapped packages into all parts of the freezer and arrange them in crisscross fashions so air may circulate freely. This speeds the freezing process. When rearranging for final storage stack packages close together for space saving, and label side up for quick identification.

Another good trick for identification is to store frozen meat by category. I often store venison and big-game roasts on the shelf harboring the most space in my upright freezer. Flat cuts such as chops and steaks supply the next highest volume, so they go in the second largest area. Next comes burgers and small chunks which I freeze in Ziploc bags. These packages go into wire baskets that keep the frozen bags from sliding all over. Soup bones go into door compartment. I usually reserve the top shelves for frozen vegetables from my garden. This system enables me to find what I want to cook in a hurry, and it allows me to quickly inventory what I have left in any given category in either of my two freezers.

That's why I favor upright freezers. Chest freezers are cheaper to operate, but it's considerably more difficult to locate specific packages in them. With the chest freezer the cold settles down on contents when the lid is opened. With the upright the cold air spills out and is wasted. Odd-shaped packages also tend to fall out of uprights if they're not stacked correctly or stored in wire baskets.

To insure top quality freezing either type should maintain a minimum of 0 degrees F. Never underbuy in size. For storage, figure four-cubic feet of frozen food per person. So if you have four hearty eaters in your family you'll want at least one 16-cubic foot unit. If you get a lot of fish and game, raise a lot of vegetables, and take advantage of special buys in supermarkets you should figure at least six cubic feet of freezer storage per family member.

Always buy freezers slightly larger than you think you'll need. I have two uprights totaling 28 cubic feet, and there is usually overflow frozen items in my refrigerator freezers.

By all means, buy manual defrost models. The cost of running one is considerably less than frost-free models, but of more importance is the fact that frost-free models tend to draw moisture out of frozen foods, a situation exactly opposite of what you want. During freezing water in meat is transformed into ice crystals. These ice crystals must not be removed because they should be returned to the meat as juice during thawing. Frost-free models tend to remove these crystals and promote freezer burn.

Manual defrosting isn't a big deal, but it should be done once a year. One half inch of frost indicates that your freezer is beginning to run inefficiently, and that means defrost time. I usually do it in late summer when many stocks are low, particularly game.

Wrapping or covering frozen packages with newspaper, then covering the pile with sleeping bags will keep the food frozen for many hours. After defrosting, wash the insides of your freezer with a mixture of warm water and baking soda. Wipe dry before replacing food.

Some general tips should help. Use a refrigerator-freezer thermometer for frequent checks on your freezer's calibration. When I'm away from home for extended periods I put two ice cubes on a shelf in plain view. If the cubes are still there when I return I have the peace of mind of knowing that the freezer operated perfectly while I was gone.

Don't overlook the advantages of freezing cooked meals. One-pot meals, particularly casseroles, are always winners. Any and all big-game meats are ideal for casseroles, but be sure to make them with vegetables that freeze well. Biggest no-no is the potato, it always turns mushy after thawing. Don't put in seasonings or cheese either, because freezing may change their flavor. Add potatoes and seasonings after you thaw the casserole. To cook twice is to overcook, so it's best to cook the original dish a bit less than the time the recipe calls for. Freeze it, then finish the cooking after the dish is thawed.

Casseroles are a great way to use odds and ends from your freezer. A hunting friend recently cleaned out his freezer and made a big casserole out of game and vegetables. He used various parts of deer and elk; plus onions, green pepper, tomatoes, mushrooms and broccoli (all vegetables that freeze well) then froze several packages of the casserole. Freeze meal-size packages.

The convenience of frozen one-pot meals is great for camping hunters. Each member of the group prepares and freezes several meals of his choice at home. When leaving for camp the frozen packages are stowed in a cooler, acting in place of ice to keep other foods cool during travel time. They won't thaw completely for at least two days, and even then they'll keep in the cooler for three more days of safe storage time. Each evening's meal is prepared with little more effort than dumping package contents into a deep pan and heating. An added touch is covering casserole contents with thick gravy, which also freezes well. Other one-pot meals that are great for freezing include meat loaf and stews.

You can keep air exposure to frozen meat to a minimum by planning a week's meals in advance. Remove all the food you're going to cook at the same time, and place it in the freezer section of your refrigerator. This system allows getting many meals out of the freezer by opening it only once.

With all meats, the general rule is that larger pieces stay frozen better than small ones. Cook small, cut up pieces of game early in the freezing year. Save larger roast for later meals.

Don't use wax paper for freezer wrap, but it's great to put between chops, burgers and other cuts that need to be separated during defrosting. Little sections of freezer paper will serve the same purpose. You can separate individual pieces from the same package — even while they're still frozen hard — by forcing a knife blade between the pieces and prying apart. Rewrap the balance. This works only if the pieces are separated by paper. It's a great convenience when you want to cook only part of a package of frozen meat. Freezing packages of several cuts also promotes efficient freezing because the inside cuts are never subject to air. Since moisture escapes from each cut surface, smaller packages lose more moisture than bigger ones.

Knives ---
Your Most Important Tools

To some people, a knife's a knife: As long as it cuts reasonably well it's good enough. At the opposite extreme are cooks who fully understand the enormous benefits of well designed and truly sharp knives. Once you work with a knife that's designed for the cutting job at hand you'll slice many hours off a year's worth of cutting and carving meat.

It's impossible to overrate a good knife. Chuck Williams, founder of the Williams-Sonoma chain of cookware stores, is the man behind those beautiful catalogs that make us want to rush out and buy more equipment for our already overstocked kitchens. Williams say all you really need to prepare a meal is a good knife and a pot.

"I have always told people to buy only the kitchen equipment they know they will use many times," adds Williams. "Every cook uses knives and pots more than anything else. You'll never regret it if you buy good equipment."

However, it's easier to go overboard on knives than any other item of kitchen cookware. When I first started cooking I figured the knives in my wife's kitchen were standard equipment and probably as good as most average cooks used. And they were. If you don't butcher your own venison you likely don't need any better knives than are already in your kitchen, and you can go on to the next chapter without missing much. But if you're really serious about butchering a lot of wild meat the following information should help you a great deal.

A really sharp knife should glide right through the meat with no dragging. The sharpest possible edges give the cook the pleasure of complete cutting control combined with less cutting effort. The best quality knives are designed for perfect balance. They feature comfortably contoured handles engineered to give a firm grip when wet. The best handles are those made of textured rubber, fused or molded polypropylene, or rubberlike compounds. In addition to featuring the best grips, these handles resist the long-term effects of water, blood and other meat juices.

It's not enough in the 90s to say that the best knife blades are made of stainless steel. That's not true today. They very best are forged from extraordinarily tough high carbon stain-resistant (not stainless) alloys developed in aerospace engineering. Edgecraft Corporation makes their knives from the unique Trizor steel. The company claims that Trizor steel guarantees an edge that lasts up to 10 times longer than some of the traditionally best European or domestic kitchen cutlery.

Yes, you get what you pay for. But only when you know what you're looking for. You don't need a lot of knives. I do 95 percent of my butchering with only two knives, a 6-inch utility knife and a 5.5-inch boning knife; both manufactured by Edgecraft Corporation, P.O. Box 3000, Avondale, PA 19311-0915. (1-800-342-3255) These knives (about $55 each retail) are by far the best I have ever worked with.

Besides not needing a lot of knives, hunters should forget the macho routine about the bigger the better. A 6-inch blade will handle any venison-cutting job. And you don't need a heavy knife. Big blades do nothing more than add unneeded weight. Shop where you can remove the knife from its packaging. Feel the handle in your hand while holding he knife firmly. Does it fit and feel comfortable? Various manufacturers have various handle designs. Buy one that feels right for your hand. Heft

Knives - Your Most Important Tools

it in different cutting positions. Pretend you're using it. Find one that feels good, but don't buy it until you determine the quality of the blade. With good care a 20-dollar knife could last for many years, a 50-dollar knife could last for generations. Don't scrimp on quality for 20 bucks or so.

If you pay a lot of money for a knife then find that the blade stains consider yourself lucky. That's a trait of top quality high-carbon steel. Beware of true stainless steel knives. They are too brittle for sustaining hard work, and stainless does not take an edge easily. Neither does any knife that doesn't have a steady taper from the thick top side all the way down to the cutting edge. A blade that's thick all the way through except for a small cutting edge becomes almost impossible to sharpen after relatively little use.

True stainless is fine for field-dressing chores where most cutting is through skin and muscle and easy-cutting meaty areas. Great convenience is experienced with a folding knife featuring a locking device that locks the blade open. The smaller ones, incorporating 2 1/2 - 3-inch blades, can be carried easily and comfortably in a pocket and are excellent tools for gutting deer. I recall paying about $5 many years ago for the one I still use. It hasn't failed me yet and it has field dressed scores of deer. The trick is in sharpening it after every gutting job.

Use of a folding knife in the field and non-folding full-tang knives in the kitchen is the best way to go. If you must have a knife on your belt, go with a folding type. It's a better deal than carrying a knife in a pocket. Always look for quality construction, especially a blade that locks in position with no trace of wiggle or sloppiness.

Knife shoppers always hear that "full-tang" knives offer the best quality. A full tang extends all the way to the end of the handle and can be seen on riveted-handle knives. A full tang is no guarantee of quality, but it's important because it's the only thing that counterbalances the blade. You have to have physical balance for best flexibility. That's why, again, you should buy knives that feel right for your hand. You probably won't find one that's comfortable unless it's full-tang.

Okay, so what will I have to pay for a knife that should last a lifetime? At the very high end are knives with ceramic blades. They are made from zircon oxide. The only harder materials are diamonds. You'll have to pay well over $150 for one of these knives, a totally unnecessary expense. Next comes the relatively high-priced knives like Edgecraft, then long popular Buck Knives that retail in the $35 to $50 range. You can be reasonably sure of getting fine quality steel knives if you select one for about $40.

For much of my butchering career, sharpening knives was a struggle. I'll guess I had read dozens of pages of instructions on how to hone blades, but I never became really good at the job. I finally developed a system of using whetstones. With a little work I could always get a knife sharp enough so that the blade would hang up when drawn very gently over a fingernail. I figured such a blade was about as sharp as possible. That was before I met Sam Weiner, President of Edgecraft Corporation. "A sharp knife is a safe knife because you know it's incredibly sharp and you respect it," Sam told me. "Properly sharpened knives will be much sharper than any knives you have ever worked with, and must be handled with extreme care. Do not run a finger or thumb along an edge to determine sharpness. To do so is to invite a serious wound."

Knives that sharp will reward you with many years of superior cutting performance in a fraction of the time normally required. Butchering becomes more of a pleasure than a chore.

There are several sharpeners on the market, each with their own claims about being the last sharpener you'll ever need. Good diamond whetstones retail in the $20 bracket. For a little more money — the $30 to $60 range — you can get sharpening systems featuring attachments that maintain constant blade angles. These knife/clamp angle guides assure efficient sharpening strokes. I'm partial to the Diamond Hone electric sharpeners manufactured by Edgecraft. The top of the line model, about $80, features three different diamond-grit wheels. The sharpener hones and polishes the entire length of a cutting edge in three steps.

Each station on the sharpener has strong magnets that hold the knife blade at the precise angle for precision sharpening. An economy model, about $48, is a two-stage sharpener. Since I got my unit I've been amazed at how simple knife sharpening has become. This sharpener provides a foolproof way to get the job done. A mechanical sharpener can

Knives - Your Most Important Tools

be one of the best investments you'll ever make if you do a lot of butchering. If you don't, you can probably get by with one of the newer ceramic stones sharpeners. Cabela's introduced one in 1995 for $13.95. Used properly, these stones do a surprisingly good job of keeping knives sharp.

I've experimented with several knives having the serrated blades touted as "never needs sharpening." The better quality designed in the $8 to $10 range do a reasonable cutting job on some foods like grapefruit, vegetables or hard cheese, but they're not worth much for cutting meat. The blades grab meat tissues, they provide much less control for clean slicing, and they produce uneven, less refined cuts.

Any good chef will tell you that a sharp knife is a surer implement. How do you tell if a knife is really sharp? The best test I know is drawing the blade over a just-ripe tomato. A sharp knife will cut the skin by its own weight. A sharp knife will also slice effortlessly through a piece of closely held newspaper with the lightest drawing motion.

Good butchers prefer to keep a knife continually sharp with use of a sharpening steel. Before each use they briefly stroke the blade's edges across the steel. Hold the base of the blade against the round steel at the angle at which it was originally sharpened. Draw the knife toward you in an arc from base to tip. Repeat on the other side. Alternate sides until the blade is sharp. While a sharpening steel actually won't sharpen a dull knife by removing metal from the blade, it does realign the edge and helps keep a sharp knife sharper longer. That's why butchers use them every few minutes during cutting sessions.

It's fascinating to watch good butchers in action. They make sharpening knives and slicing precise cuts of meat look simple. Butchering a deer always is much easier after you have watched an expert take the mystery out of the job. Fortunate is the hunter who has watched a friend cut up deer a few times. You learn in a hurry when you can watch how the cuts are made.

Now anybody can get a superb education in this art for only $29.95. That's how much you'll pay for the video "BIG GAME Field to Table." This is Jerry Chiappetta's superb production that shows exactly

Best Venison Ever

how to field dress and butcher a deer. Every cut is shown in precise detail. This video is by far the best I have ever seen on the subject. To order your copy call toll-free 1 800 819-3799, or write WILD HARVEST VIDEOS, 4241 Cherry Hill Drive, Orchard Lake, MI 48323.

Ways To Cook Tough Meat

Cooking in a crockpots, cooking in liquid — or both — work pure magic on the tougher cuts of lean venison. These methods slowly release the meat's natural gelatin, which in turn transforms the toughest venison into succulent and deliciously tender meals.

Slow cooking also makes preparation easy, so easy that it's my idea of fast food: things you can make ahead and then heat up in minutes. There's a nutritional bonus to cooking and then refrigerating, too. Before reheating, the congealed fat can be lifted off and discarded. Slow cooking is a bonanza for working people who don't have much time for the kitchen except on weekends. It's also perfectly suited to extract and unite the flavors of fresh vegetables and less tender cuts of meat at the same time.

When purchasing any crockpot type cooker it's best to go with quality. Look for models with glass tops. Plastic covers don't retain even temperatures nearly as well. Some units come with roasting racks, others don't, but these racks have distinct advantages. Fatty cuts cooked on a rack allow fat to drip into the bottom of the cooker. This is especially desirable when the meal is cooked with vegetables. The rack prevents all foods from absorbing fatty liquids. Most multipurpose cookers are round, but I prefer the oblong types that are shaped like the things I want to cook; a large rump roast for instance. An oblong shape also neatly accommodates two sandwiches for grilling, or several long pieces of bacon, etc.

Try this simple recipe for a very lean chuck or blade roast.

> 3 to 4-pound venison roast
> 2 tablespoons diced onion
> 1 teaspoon seasoned salt
> 1 teaspoon seasoned pepper

Place roast in bottom of pot, no rack. Sprinkle other ingredients on meat. Cook on low for about 6 hours. At this point you have excellent sandwich meat when roast cools enough to cut. For a full meal add chunked onions, potatoes and carrots. Cook another two hours.

RUMP ROAST #1

> 4 to 5-pound roast
> 1 16-ounce package of frozen stew vegetables
> 1 small package fresh mushrooms, sliced
> Seasonings to taste

Place roast in bottom of pot with rack. Season meat, cover with layer of mushrooms. Surround meat with thawed vegetables. Cover pot, turn heat to low, cook for 9 hours. Dinner will be almost ready when you get home from work. Drain liquid from pot for gravy, return all other ingredients to pot to keep warm. When eating, sop gravy with robust French bread.

RUMP ROAST #2

> 4 to 5-pound roast
> 6 uncooked bacon strips
> 1 large onion, sliced
> Seasonings to taste

The secret is to top the roast after seasoning with a layer of bacon. This allows a slowly-released fat source to simultaneously baste, flavor and tenderize while inhibiting shrinkage. Begin by seasoning roast, then put on rack in pot. Surround sides of roast with sliced onions. Cover the top of meat with bacon strips . . . or substitute a thin layer of beef fat.

Cook on low for 6 to eight hours. Serve with quick vegetables, such as asparagus, corn or snap beans. Get a bonus by covering mashed potatoes with gravy made from drippings in pot.

SAUCY ROUND STEAK SUPPER

This is a great recipe to use if you discover the steaks from your huge trophy buck are well on the tough side.

2 to 3-pounds of 1 1/2 inch thick round steaks
1/2 cup chopped onion
1/2 cup chopped celery
1 8-ounce can mushroom stems, drain and reserve liquid
1/2 cup French dressing
1 2 1/2-ounce package sour cream sauce mix
1/2 cup water
1 teaspoon Worcestershire sauce

Cut meat diagonally into 1/4-inch strips and place in pot. Add onion, celery and mushroom stems. In small bowl, combine salad dressing, sour cream sauce mix, water, Worcestershire sauce and reserved mushroom liquid. Pour over mixture in pot. Simmer for 5 to 6 hours. Serve over noodles or mashed potatoes. Makes about 6 servings.

MEATBALLS WITH RICE

This is another excellent recipe for utilizing meat from a tough old buck. Grinding the meat into burger is the first step in tenderizing, slow cooking adds the finishing touches.

1 pound venison burger
1/2 cup cracker crumbs
1/2 cup milk
1 egg
3 tablespoons minced onion
1/2 teaspoon salt
1/4 teaspoon basil
3 tablespoons flour
1 pound frozen tomatoes-thawed

1/2 cup sliced onion
1 cup raw rice

In mixing bowl, combine burger, cracker crumbs, milk, egg, minced onion, salt and basil. Form into about 12 meatballs. Roll in flour. Set aside.

Place tomatoes in pot, break up with a spoon to cover bottom of pot. Cover with sliced onions and sprinkled salt. Place meatballs on top on onion slices. Simmer for 5 to 7 hours. One hour before serving add rice and stir to bottom of pot. Cook at medium for one more hour. Serves 4 to 6.

TOUGH-VENISON STEW

Stewing tough meat always helps to tenderize, but slow cooking for an extra long time does an even better job.

3 pounds venison stew meat, cut into 1 1/2-inch cubes
1 cup chopped onions
2 garlic cloves, minced
6 cups water
4 beef bouillon cubes
1 1/2 lbs. potatoes, pared, cut into 1/4-inch slices (3 cups)
1/4 teaspoon celery seed
1 20-ounce package frozen peas
1/2 cup flour

Put all ingredients except peas and flour into pot. Season to taste and sprinkle on 1/8 teaspoon thyme. Simmer for 8 to 10 hours. Check meat for tenderness during last couple of hours. When cubes are almost tender, add peas and stir in flour. Raise heat enough to get new simmer, cook for one more hour. Makes 8 to 10 servings.

SLOW-COOKED CHILI

2 pounds ground venison
1 1/2 cups chopped onion
1 cup chopped green pepper
2 garlic cloves, cut finely

Ways To Cook Tough Meat

2 pounds frozen tomatoes, or 1 28-ounce can whole tomatoes
2 16-ounce cans kidney beans
2 tablespoons chili powder
1 teaspoon cumin
Seasonings to taste

Brown ground venison on range-top, then place in slow cooker. Add onion, green pepper, garlic, tomatoes, kidney beans, salt and pepper to taste, chili powder and cumin. Stir to combine. Cover and simmer for 7 to 9 hours. Makes 8 to 10 servings.

There are many recipes in many cookbooks utilizing ground venison. Always remember that thorough grinding of tough meat is guaranteed to help tenderize it, and slow cooking in liquid continues the process. One of my best deer-hunting buddies doesn't even bother trying to get tender steaks and chops from a tough buck. As soon as he determines that the animal is far from prime he has all the remaining meat ground into deer burger. Other veteran hunters I know don't go quite that far. In addition to burger, they use the toughest cuts for stews, soup, jerky, sausage, chili, etc., all are cooking methods that help tenderize.

Braising is still another way to go. It's an old technique that also uses liquid and low heat. It is a long, slow cooking method that develops flavor and tenderizes meat by gently breaking down the fibers. The meat is browned first, then cooked in a tightly covered just-deep-enough baking dish or casserole to hold meat and vegetables in surrounding liquid. Enough broth or stock is used to moisten the meat but not cover it completely. Braised dishes are best made ahead, to allow their flavors to pull together while creating a mouth watering whole meal.

Braised venison dinners smack of the best home cooking, dishes that are perfect for family dinners or informal meals with friends. They're special too, because they are rarely found in restaurants. They satisfy not only in the way they taste, but also in their unusual and unique looks.

BRAISED VENISON SHANKS

4 venison shanks, knuckle removed

4 large cloves garlic, minced
1 large rib celery, strings removed, minced
2 medium carrots, minced
1 medium onion, minced
1 cup dry red wine
1 1/2 cups chicken broth
2 large tomatoes, peeled and diced
1 teaspoon dried rosemary

Rinse shanks and dry with paper towel to remove any surface moisture. Season to taste with salt and pepper. Heat one tablespoon olive oil for searing in nonstick skillet. Sear shanks until well browned all over. Transfer to casserole or baking dish large enough to hold shanks in single layer in close-fitting pattern.

Reuse skillet with another tablespoon olive oil. When hot, add garlic, celery, carrots and onions. Cook over medium high heat until fragrant and onion is somewhat tender, about 4 minutes, stirring often.

Add red wine, chicken broth, tomatoes, rosemary; a sprinkling of thyme is optional. Bring to boil. Ladle over venison shanks. Bake, covered, at 350 degrees for 1 1/2 to 2 hours; turning shanks about every 30 minutes. Add more broth if necessary to keep liquid level close to top of shanks. Meal is best if made a day or two ahead of serving so dish can be cooled. This allows the flavors of all ingredients to mellow and meld together. Also, any solidified fat is easy to remove.

To serve, reheat tightly covered at 375 degrees for 30 to 40 minutes. Serve on hot plates with exposed bone sticking up. Goes great with Fettuccine or noodles. Makes 4 servings, and each serving contains only about 300 calories. Freezes well for future fast-food dinners.

The toughest meat cuts come from the more developed muscles. These include the shoulder as well as the shanks. The shoulder cuts are very muscular, which makes them tough. They are also richly flavored, making them excellent candidates for braising, which in turn can make them fork tender.

BRAISED VENISON SHOULDER ROAST

4 pound venison shoulder roast, deboned
5 strips uncooked bacon
1/2 cup all-purpose flour
1/2 cup vegetable oil
2 cloves garlic, minced
1 quart tomatoes, undrained
1 large onion, sliced
1/2 cup chopped green pepper
2 teaspoons cumin
Venison stock or beef broth
Seasonings to taste

Insert bacon strips into areas where bones were removed. Close roast and bind with cotton twine. Dredge meat in flour. Brown in hot oil, about 8 to 10 minutes. Transfer to casserole or baking dish. Add remaining ingredients and, if necessary, enough venison stock or beef broth to surround but not cover them with liquid. Simmer for two to three hours until meat is tender. Serves 4 to 6.

Venison ribs are another great candidate for braising because the moisture and long, slow cooking process partially destroys the tough connective tissue between the bones.

BRAISED VENISON RIBS

3 to 4 pounds ribs, cut in half to make small ribs
1/2 cup all-purpose flour
1 tablespoon ground ginger
2 tablespoons Crisco
1/4 cup sugar
1/4 cup apple cider vinegar
1/4 cup ketchup
1 tablespoon Worcestershire sauce
2 tablespoons soy sauce
2 tablespoons cornstarch

Venison ribs have lots of tallow tucked under the thin slabs of connecting meat. It's important to cut away as much of this tallow as possible to eliminate the sticky taste that comes with eating venison fat. Combine flour and ginger, mix, dredge ribs in mixture. Brown ribs over high heat in Dutch oven. Remove ribs and set aside, Reduce heat to low, then add remaining ingredients. Stir and cook for about three minutes. Place browned ribs into mixture. Simmer for about two hours or until meat is tender. Stir often. If necessary, add venison stock or beef broth to maintain a surrounding — not covering — level of liquid. Makes four to six servings. Serve over rice, noodles or mashed potatoes.

BRAISING TIPS: Always use a heavy pan to maintain even heat, Get oil or shortening to high heat before beginning to brown meat. The key to braising success is paying attention to the browning operation so that the meat is evenly browned on all sides. Your cooking vessel must have a tight cover to maintain a gentle simmer.

Cooking times in recipes are approximate because deer meat varies in degrees of tenderness. You can't go wrong if you continue simmering until meat is fork tender. After browning, pour off pan drippings to eliminate even more unwanted fat. Tough cuts from the shoulder — including both arm and chuck — are great candidates for braising. So is neck meat, especially if it's from a big, rutting buck. The amount of liquid you need for braising can be minimized by selecting a braising pan that's only slightly larger than the cuts or cut of venison to be braised.

Getting The Most From Seasonal Ingredients

My appreciation of the power of fresh vegetables always peaks when I make kabobs with just picked vegetables from my garden. It's difficult to explain why this combination produces such magic, but I'll give it a try.

One time I took a venison shoulder roast from my freezer, thawed it then cut bite-size pieces of meat from the choicest section. I had more cut meat than I could use for the kabobs I was making, so I put the extra pieces in the refrigerator. Then I made the kabobs, broiled the works and sat down to a meal that was so complete and satisfying that it could be termed nothing less than superlative.

The next day my wife sauted those extra pieces of meat. They didn't measure up to the taste quality of the meat in the kabobs, even though both groups were cut from the same roast at the same time. Why? The only possible answer is that the clear, uncomplicated and delicate flavors of those super-fresh vegetables worked into the kabobs meat while cooking.

So, make a mental note that when fresh vegetables are available you can enjoy the best kabobs of the year. The following recipe calls for venison, but fine results can be enjoyed with bite-size pieces of any big game. Some of my best kabobs were made with elk meat.

    1 pound cut up venison
    1/4 cup Italian salad dressing
    2 small zucchini cut into 1/2-inch chunks
    1 green pepper cut into 1-inch squares
    1 cup large mushroom caps sliced in half
    4 medium onions, quartered
    4 medium tomatoes cut into 24 pieces (approximate)
    8 skewers

Combine meat chunks and Italian dressing in bowl or plastic bag. Marinate minimum of three hours, eight hours is better.

To assemble kabobs: Evenly divide ingredients onto skewers. Grill (on gas or charcoal) four inches from heat source for six to 10 minutes, turning twice. Side dish of tossed salad goes great. Serves four.

For inside broiling arrange kabobs on broiler pan. Set oven to broil and preheat. Broil three inches from heat source for eight to 12 minutes, turning kabobs once. Garden fresh string beans make another superb side dish.

An even faster way of achieving almost the same result is stir-frying with a wok. A good stir-fry featuring big-game meat and just-picked vegetables produces amazing taste and texture. Any big-game meat and all vegetables may be used in many combinations, so work with whatever ingredients suit your taste.

The biggest key to success is in cutting your meat in long, thin, diagonal strips across the grain. This exposes large surface areas to the immediate high heat of a wok. Quick searing keeps the meat moist and tender. The same technique holds true for vegetables. Cut them in thin strips on long diagonals.

Use any kind of vegetable oil. Animal-based oils burn too easily. Sear the meat first with a tablespoon or two of oil, then set aside. Of all vegetables mushrooms cook the fastest (about 30 seconds), and carrots the slowest, about two minutes. It's best to consult a wok cooking guide for details on how to schedule cooking times for various vegetables, but it's a sure bet that sliced mushrooms go in last. That's the time to return the seared meat slices to the wok.

Any fast cooking method retains the nutrients and character of each vegetable, without making it limp and lifeless. You don't need a wok, of course. You can enjoy the same cooking process with a cast iron frying pan or an electric frying pan. Simply set the electric unit to 400 degrees. The key to success is mostly in matching the very freshest vegetables with thin cuts of meat. In my area of Michigan the first stir-fly of the year comes about mid-May. It combines asparagus with thin strips of venison round steak.

> 1 cup onion, cut julienne
> 1 teaspoon minced garlic
> 3 tablespoons vegetable oil
> 1 pound marinated venison round steak cut in thin strips
> 1 cup sliced mushrooms
> 1 cup fresh asparagus, chunked
> 1/2 cup green or red pepper, cut julienne
> 1 teaspoon cornstarch
> 1/4 cup soy sauce

Stir-fry onions and garlic in 2 tablespoons oil in frying pan or wok over high heat until onions are translucent. Remove with slotted spoon to large bowl. Add venison to pan or wok. Stir-fry until meat is browned, about four minutes. Remove and add to onions and garlic. Put remaining vegetables and tablespoon of oil in pan. Stir-fry three to four minutes until vegetables are tender crisp. Add to mixture in bowl. Combine cornstarch and 1/4 cup water in small bowl. Add to pan along with soy sauce. Cook, stirring, until thickened, about one minute. Put ingredients in large bowl back into pan and toss with sauce. Heat through. Season to taste. Makes four large servings.

Venison chops with a large side dish of buttered asparagus makes one of the quickest and best meals of early spring. Put enough water into a large skillet to cover no more than two layers of asparagus. Bring water to a boil before adding vegetables. Cook three to five minutes, depending on size of the spears. They should be tender but still crisp. Drain quickly and brush with melted butter or margarine. Season to taste. Figure six spears of asparagus per serving. The fresher this vegetable is the greater its ability to lift any light-style meal far above the ordinary. Lucky is the big-game hunter who can walk from his home to his asparagus patch and snap fresh spears for dinner.

Peas are one of the earliest crops to mature in home gardens. Small red potatoes (if I get them planted no later than early May) will be large enough to eat about the time the peas are ready for harvest. Parsley will be ready too. Picture perfectly cooked slices of venison rump roast placed on one side of a plate, then matched with hot buttered peas and small red potatoes topped with green parsley on the other side. That's about as good as a meal can get.

By July my two gardens are beginning to produce an amazing abundance of fresh produce. One of my specialties is a zucchini casserole. It's a favorite of almost everyone who has ever tried it in my house. It's excellent with any game dinner. It's so good that I make big batches of it for freezing. The secret is that it combines three of the best vegetables into a dish that produces a superb and unique taste.

It's made with equal amounts of sliced zucchini, sliced onions and sliced tomatoes. You can make it in any size pan, skillet or heatproof casserole. The only limiting factor is the amount of vegetables you have to work with. My big garden produces zucchini and onions before tomatoes, so I use frozen tomatoes for my first batches in early summer. I slice the tomatoes when they're about half thawed. The only other ingredients are thyme, rosemary and mozzarella cheese.

Start by slicing small zucchini into roughly 1/8 to 1/4-inch pieces. Place enough on the bottom of your cooking container to form a layer two slices thick. Sliced onions make the next layer, then comes a layer of sliced tomatoes. If you are working with small onions and tomatoes, cut each slice in half. I cut bigger vegetables in thirds, or even break them up in chunks; it makes little difference as long as you produce distinct layers. Pinch a bit of thyme and rosemary on top of each layer, plus a dash of cooking oil.

The smallest batch will contain one layer of each vegetable, the

Getting The Most From Seasonal Ingredients

largest several layers of each. I usually use a big container and top it off with three layers of each. Simmer the whole works for 45 minutes to an hour. Cover the top with mozzarella cheese about five minutes before serving, it melts and spreads in a hurry.

When I cook up a batch for freezing I eliminate the thyme, rosemary and cheese because none of these ingredients freeze well. I freeze meal-size quantities in freezer bags or other containers, then mix in seasonings and cheese after thawing.

If you have your own garden there are several ways to get full value from your plot. Double cropping is a great technique. This means cleaning a crop that has been harvested or has exhausted itself and replanting with a different crop. As soon as I use my spring peas I clear the row and plant string beans. If I freeze some of the peas I have both vegetables for use in venison stews or soups in midsummer.

Succession planting is similar to double cropping. You sow vegetables at intervals during the growing season to provide a continuous harvest. One planting will come into harvest as another finishes bearing. Lettuce, beans, sweet corn and radishes should be planted at two-week intervals to maintain a long harvesting season.

A third way to ensure having fresh produce for long periods is to plant vegetables with different maturity dates. Certain vegetables are classified as "early," "midseason" or "late." This is particularly true of tomatoes and sweet corn.

Another good way to prolong the fresh-produce season is to plant some vegetables that mature in a hurry, such as beets, peas, string beans and potatoes; and others that mature much later. The last category would include carrots, cabbage and winter squash. Carrots and squash enhance any cuts of properly cooked venison. They make all meat taste better, and they make a meal prettier too. Combining cooking savvy with gardening absolutely ensures getting the freshest and tastiest ingredients.

There is another way of achieving almost the same results without gardening. Even in the city, far from most home gardens, the weekly farmers' market has come into full swing. Area farmers drive

85

their produce-laden trucks to a parking lot in the center of cities and set up their stalls one or more days each week during the growing season. Most of these markets offer a large variety of fresh vegetables you won't find in supermarkets. Farmers aren't limited to foods that must travel long distances before reaching shelves in stores. Select markets with lots of turnover, they're likely to have the freshest produce.

Thus you'll find all kinds of REAL tomatoes, crisp cucumbers and such things as just picked sweet corn and string beans. What makes this type of produce really sing is not its variety, but its sheer freshness. One time a friend from the city stopped at my home when I was slicing tomatoes I'd taken from my garden minutes before. Russ tried a slice and remarked, "this tomato is so good it tastes like an entirely different vegetable than tomatoes I buy in a store. I've had the same experience with carrots. The taste of just-picked carrots explodes with flavor."

Still another way to combine the freshest produce with prime venison is to utilize the very latest maturing crops, especially those not affected by first frost. Cabbage roll ups make a great choice.

1 large head of cabbage
2 lbs. ground venison
2 cups cooked rice
2 eggs
2 teaspoons salt
Dash of pepper
1 medium onion, sliced

Wilt cabbage leaves in boiling water. Mix remaining ingredients and place 1/2 cup of meat mixture on a leaf and roll up. Place cabbage roll ups in greased pan. Sprinkle with brown sugar. Cover and bake 1 1/2 hours at 350 degrees F. Serves 8 -10.

The last trick is learning to rely on sturdy vegetables that hold up well in storage: carrots, potatoes, onions, squash and cabbage. When these species are stored correctly they'll be great for stews, pot roasts and soups even in the dead of winter when there is so little to choose from. Varying your cooking techniques can restore imaginative touches to vegetables, making unexpectedly tasty dishes. Tip: When boiling

Getting The Most From Seasonal Ingredients

potatoes, never cover them. Using a cover gives potatoes a reheated taste.

For more tips on making great side dishes for venison dinners see the chapter on freezing. If you can't pick or buy fresh, rely on freezing some veggies that retain fresh tastes far better than others.

Tip: add frozen vegetables to stir-fry, stew, soup or casserole near end of cooking time. Some have already been blanched, others . . such as squash . . have been cooked completely. To cook twice is to overcook. Important nutrients are lost if food is overcooked.

Bits and Pieces
Of
Helpful Information

Once you make a killing shot there is no point in cutting any main arteries to bleed the animal. As soon as the heart stops pumping there is no internal pressure to force additional blood loss.

If you get a yearling deer, which is almost bound to be tender, consider putting on a real feast similar to a leg of lamb. A roasted leg of venison offers something for everyone, from rare interior cuts close to the bone to more well-done cuts on the exterior. In the following recipe, the juices from the cooked venison and potatoes make a wonderful sauce.

    1 leg of venison, about 6-8 pounds
    1 head of fresh garlic, peeled, ends removed, sliced thinly
    1 bunch fresh rosemary, washed, dried
    2 tablespoons cooking oil
    4 large baking potatoes
    Seasonings to taste
    Sprig of fresh parsley for garnish
    2 cups light stock

Bits & Pieces Of Helpful Information

Before cooking a leg of venison trim away all fat and outside connective tissue. Cut 1/4-inch slits every few inches across the surface. Insert garlic and twigs of rosemary alternately in the incision pockets. Rub cooking oil over meat so that all sides are covered. Season meat to taste.

While oven is preheating to 425 degrees, peel and slice potatoes very thinly. Place layer of sliced potatoes in bottom of large roasting dish. Repeat with other layers until all potatoes have been used. Pour stock slowly across the potatoes to moisten, not submerge.

Place venison on top of potatoes. Place roaster on lower rack of oven and cook meat 15 minutes to sear. Turn oven temperature down to 350 degrees. Cook 20 minutes per pound. Baste with broth from potatoes every 20 minutes.

When meat is cooked remove from oven and allow no more than five minutes before carving. Leg of venison goes best with green side vegetables such as snap beans or asparagus. Round out the menu with mint jelly, sprigs of fresh parsley for garnish, and good red wine to highlight such delicacies. Carve the venison perpendicular to the bone in medium slices. Spoon any juices from the roaster over the meat slices after placing on serving plates. Be gentle when cooking yearling venison. Preserve its moist and tender texture by cooking rare to medium rare. Serves six.

While field dressing any deer keep in mind that bacteria grows very rapidly in blood. Do not use leaves or grass to clean blood from the body cavity—such items are loaded with spoilage bacteria. It's best to wash out the body cavity with clean, fresh water as soon as possible. If the inside of the body is contaminated with stomach or bowel contents, or blood, the venison will take on a gamey flavor and begin spoiling within hours if the temperature where the animal is hanging exceeds 40 degrees. Be ruthless in cutting away bloodshot meat. Cut away a bit more than you think is necessary because this stuff spoils rapidly.

It is not necessary to remove the glands on your deer's legs before butchering. But if you insist on doing so it's mandatory to thoroughly wash the knife you used. Any knife used to cut off the glands will surely be contaminated with substances contained in these glands.

When butchering venison it's always best to trim off the outer white connective material. This tissue is difficult to grind and chew. It also gives your meat a gamey odor and taste. Separate the connective tissue (the white stuff) from the meat (the red stuff). The more your butchered cuts contain pure red meat the better they'll taste and more tender they'll be.

It's very important to realize that a lot of the gamey flavor of venison is in the fat. Trim as much of the fat as possible from the meat and you'll be throwing away much of the gamey flavor. Another reason for careful trimming is that venison fat, as it cools, tends to be sticky or tallowy. This is why it clings to the teeth and the roof of the mouth, a very unsavory situation that is easily eliminated by proper trimming of fat.

Because venison is a dry meat, only certain cuts such as steaks, chops, roasts and burgers can be cooked using the dry heat methods of broiling, frying, roasting and grilling. All other cuts are much more tender when cooked with the moist heat methods of pot roasting in slow cookers, stewing, making soups or braising.

When making burgers mix venison with beef instead of pork. Beef suet doesn't become rancid as quickly as pork fat, especially during long freezing periods.

There's an easy trick to use if you like your rolled roast highly seasoned. Before you roll it, season the side of the meat that will be on the inside of the roll with the seasonings of your choice. Then you'll have seasonings throughout the roll instead of just on the outside.

Work fast after cooking because even the best venison loses flavor as it cools, especially steaks and chops.

If you have found that slicing fresh meat very thinly for stir frying is difficult, try partially freezing it first. About 45 minutes in the freezer will make a chunk of venison firm but not hard. Then it's easily sliced across the grain.

It's best to use the old cutting board made of wood. In a classic case of modern misinformation, researchers have found that the wooden cutting board is a safer, more sanitary choice than the plastic boards we have been urged to use. Microbiologists at the University of Wisconsin recently found that bacteria thrived for hours on plastic cutting boards, but died within three minutes on wooden boards. The scientists suspect that moisture in the cells of bacteria are drawn into the wood fibers, killing the cells by dehydration. This discovery emphasized the possibility that your own venison butchered on a wooden cutting board may be far safer to eat than any commercial meat purchased in any market. A U. S. Department of Agriculture spokesman recently said that a single commercial beef patty may contain meat from hundreds of animals butchered on hundreds of cutting surfaces.

Almost all deer hunters I know seldom bother saving the heart. Some reject the idea of eating organ meat, but most don't want to bother with the seemingly difficult job of removing all the blood vessels and tough lining inside of the heart. There's an easy way. Slice the heart down its center. Wash each half in warm water. This washes all the blood out and makes it easier to cut out the arteries and veins.

Try venison blueburgers for a change.
1 1/2 pounds ground venison
1 small onion, peeled, finely chopped
1/2 teaspoon garlic powder. Do not substitute fresh garlic, it will burn
6 ounces blue cheese, crumbled, divided
12 drops hot pepper sauce
6 slices low-fat Muenster cheese, divided
6 buns
6 small lettuce leaves, optional

Preheat grill. Gently mix together venison, onion, garlic powder, seasonings of your choice. Form into six patties, 1/4-pound each. Place on grill. When first side reaches desired doneness, turn burgers and top each patty with 1 ounce blue cheese, two drops of spread hot sauce, and a slice of Muenster cheese. Close grill cover. Finish cooking to desired doneness and Muenster cheese is melted. Place each burger on the bottom half of bun. Top with lettuce if desired and cover with the top of bun.

Some switches on traditional meatloaf ingredients.

You can use any standard list of ingredients and cook a good meatloaf, but if you're interested in tailoring to your special tastes there are all sorts of important variables.

Best Venison Ever

1. Bread crumbs are the most common extender, but oats, rice, saltine cracker crumbs and wheat germ are all good substitutes. These ingredients absorb fat and soften the texture, and they bind wet or crumbly mixtures into a cohesive mass.

2. Add horseradish or special mustards to the mix if you like special tastes.

3. Try a layered loaf with meat, Tater Tots with onions, another layer of meat, a layer of mixed vegetables (thawed and drained) and a last layer of meat. The guide who gave me this one says it's his attempt to get the different food groups into one meatloaf.

4. If you like ham go with a small can of deviled ham worked into the mixture.

5. Wheat germ, unsalted peanuts and grated Monterey Jack cheese are excellent extras.

6. Another guide recommended refrigerating meatloaf overnight. He says this makes for perfect seasoning, and also offers a quick meal for his hunters the next day. Increase baking time by 15 minutes if loaf is put into pre-heated oven directly from refrigerator.

7. Make spur-of-the-moment chili by cutting leftover loaf into small cubes and mixing with canned red beans. Experiment until you get the combination that best suits your taste.

8. An easy trick for adding taste is mixing one cup of shredded mozzarella cheese with your other ingredients.

A Mexican friend likes his venison chops spicy. Here's his recipe for four servings.

>1/4 cup olive oil
>1/4 teaspoon liquid smoke
>1/4 teaspoon hot pepper sauce
>1 tablespoon lime juice
>1 clove garlic, minced
>4 tablespoons jalapeno jelly
>2 red bell peppers, roasted and cut into 16 strips
>8 venison chops

In a bowl whisk olive oil, juice, garlic, liquid smoke and hot sauce. Place chops in large skillet. Brush both sides with oil mixture. Cover and cook each side to about two-thirds of desired doneness, then place on ovenproof platter. Brush chops with two tablespoons jelly. Place under pre-heated broiler until glazed. Remove from oven and eat meat while still hot. Serve with a tossed salad and baked potatoes.

The average cut of venison averages just one-seventh the saturated fat of a similar cut of domestic meat. However it averages more dietary cholesterol because venison has more red muscle fiber than farm-raised meat. The net result is beneficial because the real enemy is saturated fat.

In general, the shorter the list of ingredients in any recipe the more healthful the food. For example, a whole-grain, all-natural bread can contain as few as five ingredients. A brand-name wheat bread containing preservatives, additives and artificial ingredients can have as many as 18 unnatural components. Farm-raised meat can fall into a similar category. Venison is all natural and is some of the healthiest food you can eat.

In aging venison, remember that temperature governs everything. If it is too warm, and you can't get your meat into a cooler, shorten the hanging time accordingly. There are ways to cook venison that will make even a tough animal acceptable, but spoiled meat is NOT redeemable.

When making stock for soup leave a generous amount of meat on the bones for simmering. After cooling, pick and cut into bite-size chunks before returning to liquid. Plentiful chunks of meat will turn otherwise fair soup into a superb gourmet creation.

Tender venison is extremely delicate. Its natural juices contribute almost 100 percent to its natural flavor, so it's imperative that moisture loss is kept to a minimum during high heat, fast-cooking methods such as grilling or broiling. Even a minute or two of overcooking can turn tender meat into almost unpalatable toughness. Properly preparing choice venison cuts commands a chef's undivided attention.

The Tricks With Gravy

Lumpy gravy. It was one of my biggest failings during my early years of cooking. It used to infuriate me to prepare an otherwise large and successful meal, then goof on making the gravy.

Now I know I can avoid this problem. Use the pro secret for making gravy: go with ultra-fine milled flour. If you look at regular flour under a microscope, you will see the jagged edges of the particles. When you sprinkle flour directly into hot liquid, these jagged edges stick together to form the hated lumps that can't be separated. This doesn't happen with special flours that are so finely milled the edges are polished off. These delights, such as Gravy Quick Mixing Flour and Wondra flour will not stick together.

If you don't have access to special gravy flours you can use cornstarch or regular flour. Two tablespoons will make about one cup of gravy. Use this ratio for any amount of gravy.

The first step is to get the grease out of your pan drippings. Pour them into a bowl and skim off the fat with a spoon. Return drippings to a skillet over low heat. In the same bowl mix flour or cornstarch (your gravy will come up cloudy with flour, clearer with cornstarch) with an equal amount of cold stock or water. Whisk away. Slowly blend this dissolved mixture with simmering pan juices.

That's the simple way to make gravy. There is no single right

The Tricks With Gravy

way. One popular method is returning skimmed drippings to the roasting pan set over two burners at moderately low heat. Whisk in flour until mixed. Add stock while whisking up any browned bits that are stuck to the pan until you have desired thickness. Good gravy should be smooth and have sheen. Let it simmer, stirring occasionally. It takes several minutes to cook out the floury taste.

If your gravy is too thin, add a few instant mashed potato flakes. Then simmer gently until thickened. If it's too thick slowly add more stock. Whisk or stir until you get your desired consistency.

Plain water is most apt to create bland gravy. That's why broth, bouillon, stock or even wine works better. If you want darker gravy add a dash of brown food coloring. If your gravy is too salty a touch of brown sugar can fix the problem. If gravy begins scorching it's best to dump it into another pan without scraping the bottom.

If you want to add meat or vegetables to your gravy, cook them first. Mushrooms or onions must be sauteed. Giblets must be simmered. Other things you can add are vegetable purees, herbs or seasonings. Gravy is normally served in a gravy boat. If you don't have one, put a plate under your bowl of gravy to catch spills.

If you try all these ideas and your gravy still comes up lousy, have an expert show you the tricks of his trade. That happened to me years ago. Friends called and invited my wife and I to a spur-of-the-moment hamburger cookout.

"Gee, Jeff, we'd love to come but I have a venison roast in the oven, " I answered.

"Great," Jeff replied. "Bring it over and we'll forget the burgers. I'll make the gravy, I'm an expert with that stuff."

And he is and that's how I learned.

Best Venison Ever

Go With Colorful Cooking

It is said that we eat with our eyes. Generations of cooking experts have claimed that it's very important to keep color and texture in mind when preparing main courses of food. Most average cooks never heard of this principle, but now there is proof that it can add much zest and appeal to your big-game dinners.

When the manager of a large factory in Maryland asked health consultants from Johns Hopkins University to help employees lose weight, their initial advice seemed odd: change the color of the company snack cart from bright orange to dull battleship gray, and replace the orange-and-yellow-flowered cups with plain white ones.

The changes in employee eating habits were dramatic in only six weeks. Sales at the food cart went down 40 percent. Within three months nearly 40 percent of the cart users had lost about 10 pounds each.

The exact physiological reason for this is not fully understood, but scientists believe that when light from warm colors hit the eye's retina, electromagnetic energy stimulates nerves connected to the part of the brain that controls appetite.

When I first heard about this I wondered if it was possible to come up with a meal cooked with top-quality ingredients, yet be very unappetizing. I settled on unseasoned baked whitefish, mashed potatoes, and white bread all served on a plain white plate. It looked awful.

Contrast that with a large serving platter centered with a partially-carved venison rolled roast surrounded with buttered carrots, puffed baked potatoes and springs of parsley. Next to the platter are tossed salads of crisp romaine lettuce topped with fresh sliced tomatoes.

Before I add color to those ingredients, let's go back to the consultants who claim that color can perk up appetites just as light can boost the moods of depressed people.

"Orange is the most stimulating color," claims Maria Simonson, Director of the Health, Weight and Stress Clinic at Johns Hopkins. "Yellow, red and other warm hues also prompt people to clean their plates because they promote increased appetites."

So let's put some of these colors into that rolled roast dinner. Picture the moist, juicy-pink slices of meat surrounded with steaming orange carrots, potatoes with melted butter, salad greens and slices of bright-red tomatoes. Doesn't that mental picture make your mouth water?

There are more advantages to colorful cooking. Barbara Rolls, a professor of biobehavioral health at Pennsylvania State University, says: "When you eat a particular food at the beginning of a meal it can look great, smell great and taste great. But as you eat as much as you want of particular foods their sensory properties decline. The importance of this phenomenon is that you should switch foods, food colors and cooking methods often to maintain great appetites."

Flavors can be intensified and enhanced with colorful herbs and spices. More textural variety, contrast and color will encourage varied appetites. Herbs and spices also promote changes to foods that promote consumption of a variety of nutrients, the healthiest way to eat.

Jams and jellies should be used to make an attractive glaze on many cuts of venison. They contain no fat, and they add a lovely appetizing color that bakes on during cooking. My favorite is red currant jelly, it goes well with all dark-meat game.

"Look before you cook," is cooking teacher Ann Willan's advice. "Cooking is a practical skill that's absolutely asking to be seen. You want to be able to visualize what color a dish should be when it's cooked to the correct crispness. This principle is so important that I've written 12 books in a series titled LOOK AND COOK."

So how do you visualize the best color ingredients for your venison dinners. Ideas are everywhere. Supermarkets are full of packaged and/or frozen dinners. Manufacturers of these food products pay big bucks for the enticing dinner photos that grace their colorful packages. Cooking magazine editors also hire professional food photographers to style the most appealing color photos of the best possible dinner combinations. The same goes for editors of expensive cookbooks. You don't have to buy these publications. Just take a few moments occasionally to glance through them for specific ideas of matching your meat selections with colorful vegetables and side dishes.

You'll note that many of these photos highlight the very freshest and most colorful vegetables and fruits. The old saying that fresh is best is true in more ways than just taste, it also means ultimate color. Fresh, or fresh frozen vegetables are far more colorful than canned or pickled. The successful deer hunter who has his own vegetable garden has the makings of the most appealing game dinners.

Marinades Make A Big Difference

Venison cuts that tend to be dry and tough are always helped with marinades. These liquids have the twin advantages of tenderizing and adding flavor at the same time. When you find a marinade that suits your taste you'll be adding a subtle flavor to your meat without needing sauces or additional toppings.

The job of any marinade is to transform tougher cuts of meat into succulent and deliciously tender food. But don't make the mistake of using marinades on only cuts from the neck, shoulder and shanks. I marinate all round steaks and roasts. No matter how tender these cuts may be they'll become more tender with marinating.

This procedure uses acids such as wine, milk, vinegar, tomato, orange and lemon juices to soften the fibrous tissues within meat's muscular structure. Allow about 1/2-cup marinade for each two pounds of meat. Marinades will flavor meat within an hour, but they take much more time to tenderize; at least four hours for steaks and thin roasts. Overnight is better. But don't marinate longer than 24 hours or your meat may become mushy. Marinating longer than 15 hours may make food too pungent. After many years of experimenting I've settled on 6 to 12 hours as ideal for meat 1 1/2-inches thick or thicker.

Marinating all cuts in suitable-size plastic bags makes the job and cleanup easiest. Use a bag that's large enough to hold the meat in a flat position. Always marinate in the refrigerator, never at room temperature where bacterial activity may take place. Never underestimate the power of a marinade. Remember that kabob or other cube cuts will tenderize much faster than large cuts such as thick steaks or roasts. Choose your type of marinade carefully because the acids in their makeup can be spicy or strong tasting. My family happens to like Italian salad dressing. The Wish-Bone liquid blend makes an ideal marinade. Buy it in almost any grocery and use it right out of the bottle.

Lawry's makes a variety of meat marinades. They're all great, but be sure to pick a flavor you like. There are many other brands of bottled marinades. If you can't find any you like try red wine, it was the first tenderizer that cooks used. The alcohol in wine draws out a bit of the moisture, but it is excellent for tenderizing without the use of any chemicals. If you don't like wine but still want a quick marinade use a mixture of three parts cooking oil to one part vinegar. Dried salad seasonings can be added for flavor.

Some cooks go to great effort to come up with marinades they much prefer to commercial varieties. Here are some of the most popular recipes I've heard about.

MARINADE FOR LARGE ROASTS

1/2 cup dry red wine
1/2 cup cider vinegar
1/4 cup vegetable oil
2 bay leaves
1 crushed clove garlic
2 slices onion
A dash of hot pepper sauce

TOMATO JUICE MARINADE

1/2 teaspoon garlic powder

1 tablespoon Worcestershire sauce
1/2 pint tomato juice
2 small onions, diced

TOMATO-BEER MARINADE

1 bottle of beer, small
1 cup tomato juice
1 medium onion, finely chopped
6 drops hot pepper sauce
1/4 tablespoon celery salt
Dash of garlic powder

LEMON-GARLIC MARINADE

1/2 cup lemon juice
1/2 cup vegetable oil
2 teaspoons dried oregano leaves
1 teaspoon mustard

This last one is a cooked marinade. Combine all ingredients and heat until bubbly. Cool to room temperature before using.

Use the same procedure with any marinade when treating any flat meat. Place the food into the plastic bag in level position. Pour on enough marinade to cover top side. Rub in. Turn meat over and repeat. Seal bag. Turn occasionally during marinating period because this helps keep the juices in best contact with the meat. Roasts are best marinated in glass bowls. Rub in marinade.

Remove the meat from bag and wipe off any excess marinade when ready to cook. This eliminates too much marinade taste on the surface. Cook with the same techniques you would use for unmarinated meat. Do not reuse marinades because of possible bacteria associated with raw meat.

During my marinade discussions with various game cooks, one theme came up several times. These folks claim that most commercial marinades aren't suitable for venison because they don't contain bur-

Best Venison Ever

gundy or juniper berries. I don't subscribe to that theory, but if it sounds good to you go with 1/2 cup burgundy and 3 crushed juniper berries when you mix your next batch of marinade.

Try the following marinade as a special for venison only. I got the recipe -- and a sample -- from Ed Potkey. He said it does a poor job on beef because of a different texture of meat. It did a great job on the kabobs I made from a mule deer buck Ed shot in New Mexico.

    1/2 cup cooking oil
    1/2 cup soy sauce
    1/4 cup sherry
    2 tablespoons brown sugar
    1 1/4 teaspoons dry mustard
    1 clove garlic, crushed
    1 tablespoon crushed ginger
     or 1/2 teaspoon powdered ginger

Mix well and use with 4 to 5 pounds of venison. Marinate overnight. Ed said to use Kikkoman soy sauce if you can get it. He also said to cut the ingredients in half if you are going to cook enough meat for only 2 or 3 servings.

Where There's Smoke There's Flavor

Smoke cooking is the slow, delicate technique that turns otherwise tough-texture meat into pure tenderness. In the process it produces a rich concentrated flavor that is thoroughly satisfying on its own, thereby eliminating any need for heavy sauces or other add-ons. Smoking, when done with imagination and carefully chosen ingredients, can produce the most unique tastes in the world of cooking.

In fact, smoke cooking is practiced around the world, and has been for thousands of years. Most every country and region has its smoked specialties, a true tribute to this time honored method of preparing food. Food is usually smoked not to preserve it but to impart flavor from local species of wood. Smoking is also a valuable technique in the fight against fat. Like steaming and grilling, it is a no-added-fat cooking method.

Smoked foods, once found mostly in trendy restaurants and high-priced gourmet shops, are now being produced at home with remarkably simple tricks of the trade. Before getting into the how-to-do-it, it's best to understand the advantages of why it's done. Slow, low-temperature cooking with smoke, around 180 degrees to 220 degrees, allows the tougher connective tissues of venison to soften and turn gelatinous. This results in tender, juicy meat which is specially flavored with your personal choice of wood.

In addition, smoking works best with the large, thin cuts of venison such as ribs, briskets and shoulders. This is true because smoke doesn't penetrate deeply. Smoking will enhance the flavor of the thicker cuts of roasts, sirloins and tenderloins, but will not add anything to the texture. Generally, thoroughly smoke cook the thinner cuts to tenderize, but serve the thicker cuts cooked medium rare.

The only tricky aspect to smoking is determining when the food is done. Smoked meat may remain pink at the bone even when fully cooked. It's best to use an instant-read thermometer to make sure that a safe internal temperature has been reached. Use a thermometer in this way for all smoking.

Your backyard barbecue grill will get you started into smoke cooking. It's almost ideal for accomplishing the very simple principal of exposing meat to the magic of smoke in a vented enclosure with a suitable heat source...which, in this case, is charcoal. The first decision to make is whether you want to do wet smoking or dry smoking.

A dry smoker utilizes a very hot fire. Its advantage over a wet smoker is that it cooks meat rapidly, almost like regular grilling. It involves no more that putting wood chips on your cooking fire. A wet smoker employs a pan of water between the heat source and the meat. It keeps you meat moist, which helps tenderize, and it doesn't require the cook's constant attention as does a dry smoker because the cooking process takes longer.

Your next step is determining what type of wood you'll use to produce smoke and flavor. Hardwoods and fruitwoods are best. What you use may be limited to what's available in your area. I have apple, peach and pear trees on my property, and they're all great for smoking. I favor apple simply because I like the taste of apples better than other fruits. In the south, chunks of hickory are favored. In the west most smokers go with mesquite.

Chunks of wood for smoking can be most any size up to about 1 x 2 inches. Small branches can be snipped into any lengths under six inches, bigger branches can be cut to length, then split. Soak wood chunks in water for about an hour before using. That way they'll burn slowly when you throw them on the charcoal. As a general rule, use wood chunks when smoking 3 or more hours, chips for less time.

Although wood is your main source of flavor, you can also help by adding flavor to your water pan. Put in two or three beef bouillon cubes and a few slivers of garlic, or whatever suits your taste. One of my cooking friends uses wine and honey. Whatever you add it's best to have your water pan about three quarters full. Marinades always add flavor no matter what cooking method you use. Use the same marinades you use on steaks and roasts, and use them in the same way.

Begin your smoking session by building a mound of charcoal briquettes on one side of your fire grate. Start the fire and allow it to build until the coals are white, then level mound. Spread dampened wood chips or chunks over hot coals and start the smoke rising. Open top and bottom vents slightly to keep fire going. Place the meat to be cooked on the top grate on the opposite side of the grill from the fire. Most meat smokes 2 to 6 hours, depending on size, temperature and preferred level of doneness.

Patience is the secret to success with wet smoking. Keep the temperature consistently low at about 200 degrees. Check occasionally with an instant thermometer, or place an oven thermometer on the top grate. Add charcoal to maintain the heat source when necessary, plus a few wood chips to keep the smoke strong. Control the fire's intensity by adjusting the air vents. Don't rush. Be observant of the fire, heat, smoke and cooking. The water pan should be on the grate above the coals. If the liquid gets too hot, move the pan sideways of the coals.

Don't open your wet smoker more than you have to to check on things, and don't open it at all during the first hour of cooking time. It takes that long to build up the heat and moist smoke you need. How long to smoke depends on the size of the meat you're smoking and the temperature of your fire. A thin rack of ribs may be thoroughly smoke cooked in 1 1/2 hours, a thick brisket may take 3 to 5 hours. Again, an instant-read thermometer always tells when a safe internal temperature has been reached. Safe smoke-cooking temperatures are the same as other cooking methods; about 140 degrees for rare, 150 degrees for medium, and 165 degrees for well done.

Smoking with a covered barbecue grill is an imprecise cooking technique and requires a need to experiment. Weather, in particular, can greatly affect backyard cooking times. Cold, windy days makes it difficult to maintain steady and adequate heat. On such days you'll have to use more charcoal than on still, warm days. On still days that are very cold, you'll have to open the vents more to maintain adequate heat, which in turn calls for frequent additions of charcoal.

The more wood you use, the smokier you food will taste. Hardwoods, such as maple, hickory and alder often produce slightly less smoke than fruitwoods. Each source contributes a different flavor. So, again, you'll have to experiment until you find the smoking combinations that best suit your tastes. Do not use pine or other softwoods, they'll add a pitch taste to your food.

If you're like most serious deer hunters you'll try grill smoking enough times to determine if you really enjoy smoked venison. If it turns out that you think smoked meat is great you'll probably want to invest in a commercial home smoker. Luhr Jensen's Little Chief and Big Chief models have probably cooked more backyard smoked meals than any other portable home smoker. Char-Broil and Brinkman offer models that also do great jobs. The Deluxe Charcoal Outdoorsman, manufactured by Coleman and sold in K-Mart stores, is top quality equipment and retails for about $50.

Most large sporting goods stores carry smokers, plus wood chips and/or wood chunks cut specifically for backyard smoking. Hunting and fishing equipment catalogs usually list smoke-cooking equipment. The fact that these cookers are sold in so many places is a tribute to their popularity.

The Latest Thoughts On Jerky

Homemade jerky is a great way to utilize scrap pieces of meat left over from butchering operations. It's also an excellent way to eat venison on the spur of the moment without worrying about preparing whole meals. Many successful deer hunters don't bother making jerky because it's usually a thankless job involving too much work with too many details.

If this has been your approach you should know there are modern ways to make jerky that eliminate a great deal of the traditional work. Pacific Mountain Farms sells ingredient packages that take all the work out of making the usually complicated marinades. All you do is mix this stuff with cold water, add your strips of cut meat, then refrigerate the works for about 24 hours. After that, only the drying operation remains. Get details by calling 1 (800) 647-0996, or writing Pacific Mountain Farms, RD 2, Box 354, Canisteo, NY, 14823.

The single most time-consuming job in making traditional jerky is cutting the meat into thin strips. Most published accounts say to cut the strips 6-inches long, by 1-inch wide by 1/4-inch thick. This immediately eliminates a lot of scrap meat that isn't big enough to cut to these dimensions. Also, slicing slippery meat to such thin measurements is difficult and time consuming at best. You can cut down on the time by partially freezing the meat which makes it easier to slice.

Best Venison Ever

Or you can forget the whole tedious process by grinding your venison scraps. This eliminates all the cutting problems associated with strip jerky. It also allows you to use all your meat scraps because nothing is too small to go through the grinder. The big drawback is that you can't use too much liquid marinade for making ground jerky. There's even a way around this problem. Go with the dry spices used in some jerky recipes, plus a very small amount of liquid. The recipe I got from a deer hunter in South Dakota calls for:

5 pounds venison scraps
3 tablespoons liquid smoke
1/2 tablespoon cayenne pepper
1/2 teaspoon garlic powder
1/2 cup kosher salt
1/4 tablespoon black pepper
1/2 teaspoon marjoram
2 tablespoons water

Rough grind meat scraps. Put remaining ingredients in a bowl and mix thoroughly. Add them a bit at a time to the ground meat while kneading the works like dough. You can do this with a liquid marinade too, but you have to guard against making the meat mushy. Don't use more than 5 tablespoons per 5 pounds of meat. The simplest recipe I've run across calls for:

5 pounds venison scraps
3 level tablespoons salt
1 level tablespoon ground pepper
2 level tablespoons sugar
5 tablespoons Worcestershire sauce

Mix ingredients and knead into ground meat. Grind again through 1/8-inch plate. Divide the mixture into 4 or 5 portions. Place each meat portion on a sheet of wax paper or freezer paper. Flatten by hand until the meat is about 1-inch thick. Now cover the meat with a second piece of paper. Use a rolling pin to flatten the meat to 1/4-inch in thickness. Peel off the top layer of paper. Then let each portion cool overnight in your refrigerator to further release and mix the flavors.

The Latest Thoughts On Jerky

Cut and separate into strips about 1-inch wide. Wipe off marinade and place strips on cookie sheet lined with foil. Oven dry at about 130 degrees for 4 to 6 hours. Then turn the strips over and continue drying for a total of 10 to 18 hours. Timing isn't critical with jerky, so drying time of an hour more or less won't matter. Oven dry until jerky reaches desired dryness.

One of my friends makes even less work out of the project by not cutting the meat mixture into strips before drying. He slides the whole works onto the foil-lined cookie sheet or broiler pan, oven dries it, then cuts it into strips with a pair of kitchen shears.

Note: The best ground-meat jerky is made from scraps containing almost no fat, and if care is taken to make sure the spices are thoroughly mixed into the meat. That's why it's best to run the mixture through the grinder a second time.

Any lean big-game meat without tendons or sinews can be used to make jerky, except that from javelina, bear or wild boar. Meat from all three of these animals must be cooked thoroughly to be safe to eat.

The Indians made top quality jerky from the loin or tenderloin, but any muscle from any place in the carcass can be used. Years ago some hunters believed that jerky should be made the day after the kill to prevent unnecessary bacterial growth. This theory has no basis in fact. Any aged meat can be used satisfactorily. So can frozen meat. Many hunters freeze chunks of meat to be used specifically for jerky. This way they can have freshly made jerky year around.

All meat used for jerky should be trimmed of fat and connective tissue. Almost all recipes for jerky call for the strips of meat to be cut with the grain. That's tradition, but it really isn't necessary. In fact, strips cut across the grain will have the same quality and be more tender. This is doubly true if you make your jerky from ground meat.

Some recipes call for drying jerky in the sun. The Indians did this by hanging meat strips from poles or the tops of huts and tepees out of reach of dogs. These practices antedate recorded history, and were common by 1000 B.C. Don't even think of doing this today. It's much more convenient and sanitary to oven dry or smoke your jerky.

Best Venison Ever

The color of finished jerky ranges from light brown to black. Color variations depend on the recipe used, and species and age of the animal. The latter two factors are related to the myoglobin concentration in fresh meat. Higher levels of this material result in darker colored jerky. So the color of your jerky may not be the same as you expected, but still could be processed perfectly.

Making oven-dried jerky with a liquid marinade begins with combining the marinade ingredients in a large nonmetallic mixing bowl. Stir to dissolve salt. Add meat strips. Cover with aluminum foil or plastic wrap. Refrigerate overnight or up to 24 hours, stirring every several hours. Heat oven to lowest heat setting. Drain and discard marinade from meat strips, then dry meat according to above instructions.

The principle in making all types of jerky is to dry the meat, not cook it. It is the moisture in meat that encourages enzyme action. Only by removing ALL the water content can jerky meat be preserved. Open your oven door to the first or second stop to allow moisture to escape. Warm moving air is what does the trick. You'll want to pick a cool day to make jerky because you kitchen is going to heat up a bit. Five pounds of fresh meat should weigh about two pounds after complete drying. Properly dried jerky will keep for months in quart canning jars, but the drier it is the longer it will last. It can be frozen indefinitely, but quality begins to deteriorate after a few months.

Some hunters much prefer smoked jerky. They soak wood chips for an hour while their smoker is heating to about 120 degrees. Meat strips are placed on racks which are put into smoker. As soon as a handful of wood chips begin to smoke the damper is adjusted almost closed. Smoked jerky usually dries in 3 to 6 hours. When it's done, it's dry but not brittle. Properly dried jerky strips crack when bent, but don't break.

Another way to oven dry jerky is to hang the meat strips from oven racks with toothpicks. Simply poke toothpicks through one end of the meat strips, then hang them in place by arranging the horizontal toothpicks over the openings in oven racks. When you do this you should put a tray under the perpendicular meat strips to catch drippings. The average oven will accommodate the hanging of about two dozen strips.

The Latest Thoughts On Jerky

There are various ways to flavor jerky. If you don't like the taste of liquid smoke you can marinate with soy sauce, Worcestershire sauce, or garlic powder. You can experiment with many seasonings and/or spices or steak sauces until you find combinations that suit your tastes.

In the old days jerky was an important item on menu lists because it kept meat preserved for months. It lost much of its appeal with the advent of refrigerators, even more when home freezers cane onto the scene. In recent years jerky has again become a popular item with the rediscovery of its unique taste. Its so popular now that beef jerky can be purchased in grocery stores, sporting-goods stores, in bars and even in gas stations. Lucky is the successful deer hunter who cashes in on this great taste treat.

ORDER BLANK

YES! Please send me the book "BEST VENISON EVER"

Name: _____

Address: _____

City: _____ St. _____ Zip: _____

Number of books: _____

Each book $9.95: _____

<u>Shipping & handling please add $2.50 per book:</u>
<u>(Michigan residents add 6% sales tax)</u>

Total: $ _____

Make check or money order payable to:

John O. Cartier
POB 68
Ludington, MI 49431

THANK YOU!

HOW TO GET YOUR DEER
By John O. Cartier

* If you want to bag your buck, you'd better be up-to-date on deer hunting! Whitetails have new tricks, mule deer are smarter, hotspots have changed, many of the best old hunting techniques don't work anymore... But with the new tactics you can score!

* Read why stand hunting is so successful today. Learn techniques for seeing deer. Learn when and how to stillhunt, stalk, drive, use other hunting methods. Discover the whitetail's and muley's new escape secrets.

* Over the years deer guns and ammo have changed greatly. Deer have changed, too. For one thing, they're hiding more and running less. Changes in their living areas and increased hunting pressure have forced both whitetail and mule deer to change their habits and their survival tactics.

* The hunters who are bagging their bucks every year are doing it by adapting their tactics to the new situation. Often they're using very different tactics than they used only a few years ago.

* Some of the best hunting tricks of the old pros don't work any more because the situations they were developed for no longer exist. But new techniques are amazingly productive! And there are plenty of deer (big ones, too!) out there for the hunter who knows how to get them.

* This new book, **HOW TO GET YOUR DEER,** brings you a tremendous amount of up-to-the-minute deer hunting information that was accumulated by the author, John O. Cartier, in extensive surveys and personal discussions with game management officials and top deer hunters in all parts of North America.

* The facts on best deer-hunting techniques that Cartier received from state game department officials "blow some large holes in many of the popular theories on how to hunt deer."

* To bag the more clever modern deer, you've got to know everything possible about his habits, traits, life style, habitat, reactions and tricks. Cartier gives you valuable facts and insights in separate chapters on whitetail and the muley.

*We've barely scratched the surface of all the valuable information on deer hunting in this fine new book. For more information on this book and when it will be available write to: **John O. Cartier, P.O. Box 68, Ludington, MI 49431**